A STUDY OF AMERICAN DEAF FOLKLORE

Susan D. Rutherford, Ph.D.

Linstok Press

4020 Blackburn Lane
Burtonsville, Maryland 20866-1167
www.signmedia.com

ISBN 0-932130-17-8

How to Order
Single copies may be ordered from **Linstok Press, 4020 Blackburn Lane, Burtonsville, MD, 20866-1667**. For credit card orders, place your order online at **www.signmedia.com** or phone **1-800-475-4756.**

Dedicated to:

the patience and generosity of Leo M. Jacobs

and the memory of Jesse O. Sawyer, Ph.D.

TABLE OF CONTENTS

A Study of American Deaf Folklore
Susan Dell Rutherford
ABSTRACT

This dissertation examines how the American Deaf community can be studied and better understood—both as a cultural group and as an oppressed linguistic minority group—through its folklore. In the process, the dissertation examines the different functions that folklore serves in the community: it acts as a metaphor for the group's experience; transmits group customs, values and behavior norms; serves as an educative tool for specific competencies; and, perhaps most importantly, establishes and maintains group identity.

Chapter I provides a brief demographic introduction to the Deaf community. It also sketches the evolution of the community's most identifying characteristic, American Sign Language (ASL), and the struggle to preserve the language and gain acceptance for it.

Chapter II examines how folklore mirrors the culture of a people. The chapter analyzes texts of an old Deaf joke, paying particular attention to how in-group humor serves to release aggression and relieve minority group anxieties.

Chapter III introduces the concept of "sign play" as a visual analog to Kirschenblatt-Gimblett and Sherzer's "speech play" and examines a number of traditional forms in ASL. The chapter details that some linguistic play is for its own sake, while other develops linguistic competence and serves to validate ASL as a language.

Chapter IV examines how folklore serves as a tool for education. The chapter looks at a long-standing folk tradition, the group narrative, and discusses its value to the community. The Deaf community is unique in that much culture and language is learned peer to peer. The special nature of the group narrative form promotes the simultaneous learning of language skills in a social situation and social skills in a linguistic context.

Chapter V presents texts of a number of traditional forms from the Deaf community—legends, jokes, skits, tall tales and slurred name signs—to examine and analyze the crucial role folklore plays in establishing and maintaining the Deaf identity.

Chapter VI recaps the examination of the Deaf community through its folklore. It has been seen that folklore serves to define and maintain Deaf identity, promote in-group norms, act as a tool for educational and social competencies, provide avenues for creative expression and validate the worth of the group and their culture. It is seen that through folk traditions the Deaf community can dismiss the stereotypical view of them as "broken hearing people" and come to see themselves as wholly functioning individuals.

PREFACE

It has been fourteen years since I wrote the original preface to this work. Given how swiftly and dramatically the world seems to change these days, there are probably many people who would quickly dismiss an academic study more than a decade old. But to consider this work outdated is to ignore the nature of folklore: what it is and what it does.

Folklore, in the words of the renowned Alan Dundes (1980), is a mirror of culture. It is an unselfconscious autobiographical ethnography. For outsiders, it provides an open window through which you can gain a better understanding of the world view and identity formation of a community. Folklore and culture evolve constantly, but they don't lose their relevance.

When I first wrote this study, I had been working in the Deaf community for ten years, as a producer and director of Deaf-related projects and as an academic researching the field. Although I am a hearing person, my personal and professional contacts put me in the very privileged position of developing close, trusting relationships with many active bearers of Deaf cultural traditions.

Those cultural traditions are what first drew me to this work. In 1977, I began collecting and analyzing examples of Deaf folklore in an attempt to better understand Deaf people and their place in society. The following year, with the support of Professor Jesse O. Sawyer, I developed and implemented at the University of California-Berkeley, a course on Deaf culture and American Sign Language. This course, the History and Culture of the American Deaf Community, which I continue to teach with guest colleagues from the Deaf community was the first of its kind in the nation and has since been duplicated at other institutions. This course also helped pave the way for a number of educational institutions and state governments to accept ASL as a bona fide language.

My nonacademic work continues to this day as well. During almost twenty-five years, it has included the production and direction of such media projects as American Culture: the Deaf Perspective, a five-part live presentation, four-part video series funded by the National Endowment for the Humanities; and Rainbow's End, a PBS television series for Deaf children; and the creation and fifteen-year production of Celebration: Deaf Artists and Performers, a sympo-sium and performance of Deaf arts at the University of California-

Berkeley. In recent years, the scope of the work has expanded to include
showcasing Deaf arts at mainstream venues and providing meaningful access for the Deaf community to Bay Area cultural institutions.

Over these years there have been numerous changes, large and small, surrounding the Deaf community. For one thing, I find I don't have to explain my profession as often. I tell people I study Deaf culture, and they understand. This is an encouraging sign that Deaf studies is a recognized and accepted field. More encouraging was the Deaf President Now protest at Gallaudet University in 1988, a watershed event in Deaf self-determination.

And there are the indications of the vitality of Deaf culture: I know of schools that now recognize the educational value of Deaf ABC stories and teach the genre in classroom settings. And I see folklore such as "the Civil War story," which used to be passed along at parties and in dorms, now spread on the Internet—a powerful tool for connecting people.

But there is also evidence that many things are fundamentally the same. Advocates of mainstreaming still oppose the proponents of bilingual/bicultural education while a new generation of Deaf kids gets caught in the middle. Controversy rages over cochlear implants, which some see as the latest technological wonder but others view as a tool for cultural genocide. And even today at one of California's two state schools for the Deaf, people are still fighting the oldest war of Deafness—whether ASL is a real language.

There is, finally, the most important thing that has not and will not change: As long as there are products of Deaf culture—Deaf people who interact with each other and who affect and are affected by other cultures—the dynamics of their relationships will come out in their folklore. And the study of that folklore will remain relevant to anyone who wants to understand what makes Deaf people a vital and unique community.

Some notes on the work itself: Visual language does not lend itself well to a two-dimensional written form. Therefore, it is prudent to explain how I found my samples and to discuss the issues of the collection, transcription, data analysis, and general intent of the material presented here.

The scope of my professional projects together with travel related to teaching and consulting has enabled me to draw from the national community. This work, thus, includes representative examples from the following: Alabama, Arizona, California, Connecticut, Florida, Georgia, Iowa, Kansas, Kentucky, Louisiana, Massachusetts, Minnesota, Missouri, Nebraska, North Carolina, New Jersey, New York, Ohio, Oregon, Pennsylvania, South Carolina, Tennessee, Texas, Utah, Vermont, Virginia, Washington, Wisconsin, the District of Columbia, and the countries of England and Australia. But this is only a small taste of the folk traditions of Deaf America. The reader is encouraged to seek videotape examples wherever possible and to regard the two-dimensional drawings contained herein as merely a sketch of the material, not a true representation of it. Only video, film, or live viewing can provide that true picture.

Many of the texts in this work were selected because of the relative availability of publicly accessible video or film examples. The reader is directed to the "Deaf Folklore" segment of the American Culture: The Deaf Perspective video series (San Francisco Public Library, 1984). This series reflected in large measure my work to that date and was, in fact, my attempt to publish in ASL before publishing a written companion volume. The reader is also directed to the Media collection at the Edward Miner Gallaudet Memorial Library at Gallaudet University, which houses many tapes from the extensive folklore collection of Simon Carmel.

The methods used to collect this data are varied. True collection in the language must be done on videotape. In most instances, recording a text in its original context is awkward and can be so intrusive as to have an impact on the material collected. A common technique I employed was to take notes on an item I would see in context, often as a member of the group, and then later attempt to re-elicit the text, generate discussion, and evoke an informant analysis in studio.

Another technique familiar to sign language researchers is the use of the portable video camera, blue backdrop sheet, and thumbtacks, which converts any room to an instant studio for collection. This is particularly fruitful at national Deaf Studies conferences or National Association of the Deaf conventions.

Collection of group narrative in context on video was impossible. Where attempts were made to re-elicit a text in studio, the material, although rich in its own right, did not replicate that of the traditional group narrative. The spontaneity of play seems to be a requisite. Hence, the discussion of group narrative is based largely on

observation of texts in context and substantial interview with Deaf
adults reflecting on their childhood participation in the genre.

My approach to translation closely follows the work of Dennis
Tedlock (1971) and that of Elizabeth Fine (1984). Texts are rendered in
a free translation in English. A formal equivalence has not been sought,
as it is my belief that an ASL text is rendered virtually meaningless in
a two-dimensional format. In general, a functional equivalence was
attempted. This involved combining my own translation with those
from the informants themselves and from interpreters familiar with the
informant. The interpreters were most often native signers—hearing
children of Deaf parents—many of whom offered insightful commen-
tary from their bilingual/bicultural perspectives. Most informants pre-
ferred that I work on the translation, and whenever possible they then
reviewed these translations. It is hoped that the synopses, discussions
of context, informant analysis, and the like will be meaningful, while
acknowledging that print cannot produce a true rendition of the text.

Concerning transcription conventions, I have chosen to use a simple gloss where possible, which appears in all caps. It should be noted
that the majority of titles used for texts are of my creation for illustrative purposes only, as none were issued by informants or commonly
exist within the community. This is also true for the labeling of genres
such as "Group Narrative," "ABC Story," "One Handshape Story,"
and "Fingerspelling Mime." Unattributed quotations throughout
denote informant testimony.

The information presented here was written consciously to be as
accessible as possible to all levels of English proficiency. My gratitude
to an understanding doctoral committee for its indulgence on this issue.

The intent of this work is to use folkloristics as a tool to illuminate
the language and culture of the American Deaf community. Such
illumination can contribute to a better understanding and acceptance
of Deaf people. It is written with profound recognition of my Deaf
linguistic and cultural inadequacies, and with enormous respect and
gratitude to the community who adopted me despite my limitations.

This work has benefited from the comments, suggestions, criti-
cisms, and wisdom of many. However, the responsibility for any
errors or failings is mine alone.

Berkeley, California   S.D.R.
August 2001

ACKNOWLEDGEMENTS

Many members of the Deaf community have freely given of their time, talents, insights and patience. Among them, I would particularly like to thank the following:

Pam Amundsen-Hauchildt, Carol-Lee Aquiline, Anne Marie Baer, Ben Bahan, Chuck Baird, Elizabeth Baird, Donald Bangs, Ph.D., Alan Barwiolek, Sandy Batten, MJ Bienvenu, Adrian Blue, Dr. Bernard Bragg, Joyanne Burdett, Dr. Byron Benton Burnes, Simon Carmel, Ph.D., S. Melvin Carter, Jr., Rhoda Clark, Charles Corey, Florita Corey, Lois Dadzie, Hazel Davis, Steven Ehrlich, Lou Fant, Larry Fleisher, Ph.D., Olin Fortney, Judy Gough, Jose Granda, Georgetta Graybill, Patrick Graybill, Ron Herbold, Marjoriebell Holcomb, Virginia Hughes, Tom Humphries, Ph.D., Ernest Ikeda, Paul Isaac, Forest Jackson, Harry Jacobs, Leo M. Jacobs, Sheila Jacobs, Jack Jason, Joanne Jauregui, Paul Johnston, Ph.D., Charles Jones, Barbara Kannapell, Ph.D., Eleanor Kraft, Linda Kuntze, Marlon Kuntze, Ella Mae Lentz, Dan Lynch, Joyce Lynch, Brian Malzkuhn, Nathie Marbury, Charlie McKinney, Zelephiene Meadows, Kenneth Mikos, Dorothy Miles, Mary Beth Miller, Freda Norman, Earl Norton, Kenneth Norton, Carol Padden, Ph.D., Carlene Pederson, David Peterson, Marie Philip, Lillian Quartermus, Elizabeth Quinn, Donnette Reins-McClelland, Eugene Rianda, Gary Sanderson, Tim Scanlon, Dennis Schemenauer, Nancy Schmidt, Howie Seago, Bernice Singleton, Jenny Singleton, Julian Singleton, Cheri Smith, John Smith, Sam Supalla, Ph.D., Ted Supalla, Ph.D., Mary Telford, Ellen Thielman, Hedy Udkovich-Stern, Clayton Valli, Al Walla, Ed Waterstreet, Charlotte Whitacre, Harry Williams, Nat Wilson, Evelyn Zola.

Thanks too, to all the teachers, counselors and Deaf children who allowed me in their world from time to time.

My appreciation to Simon Carmel for his generous efforts in making much of his substantial video collection accessible.

I am grateful to many for their assistance in translation of the texts and whose participation greatly enhanced the quality of this work. Among them are:

Suzy Bank-Schamberg, Beverly Cannon, Lou Fant, Stephanie

Feyne, Betsy Ford, Sheila Jacobs, Jack Jason, Shelley Lawrence, Jadine Murello, Rico Peterson, Nikki Rexroat-Norton, Lori Seago, Jenny Singleton, Ph.D., Cheri Smith

I am indebted to the San Francisco Bay Area Deaf community, which daily has enriched my life in general and my work in specific. It is this linguistic community that has generously shared its language and culture with me and has patiently allowed me to develop my sign skills in their midst. In this regard I would particularly like to thank Leo M. Jacobs, Freda Norman, Ella Mae Lentz and Carlene Pederson for their friendship, encouragement, insightful analysis and for caring enough to correct my signs and help me lessen my "hearing accent."

I am thankful to the members of my committee—to the late Jesse Sawyer, Ph.D., for support and encouragement that was always there; to Robin Lakoff, Ph.D., whose work and example has been an inspiration; to Robert Blauner, Ph.D., for sharing his scholarly insight and understanding of oppression and minority issues and reassuring me that I was indeed "on track"; to Eli Bower, Ph.D., whose good cheer and support over the years have been very much appreciated; and particularly to Alan Dundes, Ph.D., who is responsible for lighting the spark of excitement within me about the field of folklore and who has maintained it with meaningful and substantive guidance and encouragement. His demand for scholarship has enabled me to accomplish work beyond the scope of my anticipation and I am ever grateful to him.

I am especially grateful to my family, without whose support and encouragement this would not have been possible. For my son, Jay Bryon, a special thank you for the many helpful "magic fingers" massages, for patience in sharing a mother with her work, and for thoughtful understanding beyond his years. Most particularly to my husband, Rick Clogher, for his unflagging friendship and support; and for generously sharing his time, perceptive analysis and criticism and his truly consummate editorial skills.

LIST OF FIGURES

Permissions for the use of illustrations are gratefully acknowledged as follows: Figures 5, 6, 8, 17, 18, 19, 20, 23, 24, 25, 27, & 28, and ABC & Slurred Name Sign Texts, T. J. Publishers; in Figures 2, 3, 7, 9, Harvard University Press; Figure 13, Howie Seago and D.E.A.F. Media, Inc.; Figure 26, Dawn Sign Press; Figure 15, The National Association of the Deaf.

CHAPTER I

INTRODUCTION

The American Deaf Community—Who Are The Folk?

The American Deaf[1] community is that group of deaf and hard of hearing individuals who share a common language and culture (Baker/Padden, 1978: 4). In the United States there are over two million people who are "audiometrically deaf," that is, they are physically unable to perceive the sounds of speech. The American Deaf community, however, numbers approximately 500,000. Membership in this cultural group is based more on "attitudinal deafness" than on the actual degree of hearing loss. As Baker and Padden explain, attitudinal deafness means that individuals have, on the basis of certain characteristics, identified themselves as members of the community and are accepted by the other members (1978: 4).

This process parallels Barth's suggestion on the formation of ethnic groups where membership is determined by an individual's identification with the group and by the group, in turn, recognizing and identifying the individual as a member. The use of American Sign Language (ASL) is the major identifying characteristic of members of the Deaf community. Thus, individuals who are deaf but who do not use ASL are not considered members of the cultural group (for further discussion of the Deaf community as a cultural group see Padden & Humphries, 1988; Lane, 1985; Baker and Battison, 1980; Woodward, 1982; Meadow, 1972;

Markowicz and Woodward, 1975; and Lunde, 1960).

In addition to having a language that identifies its members, the community has another cultural characteristic in its its 85-95 percent endogamous marriage rate (Rainer, Altschuler & Kallman, 1963: 17; Schein and Delk, 1974: 34; Fay, 1898). Deaf people tend to marry other Deaf people almost exclusively. Still another characteristic, the existence of a formal societal structure within the culture, can be seen in the numerous Deaf organizations—local, state, national and international. Of particular note are the National Association of the Deaf (est. 1880) and the World Federation of the Deaf (est. 1951), which involve themselves with the problems of the deaf on national and international levels respectively. There is an American Athletic Association of the Deaf, which organizes Deaf sports and, since 1935, has assisted American participation in the World Deaf Olympics.

And there are national fraternal orders, sororities, and alumni associations, as well as numerous religious organizations and community social groups (for further discussion, see Gannon, 1980; Meadow, 1972; Jacobs, 1989). Articles of material culture specific to the community also exist, such as telecommunication devices (TDDs) and flashing light signaling devices to take the place of doorbells, clock alarms, and telephone rings. There are even sound-activated signal lights to alert parents to a baby's cry.

All of the above characteristics define the group, but nothing so much as the language. Roughly ten percent of the community's population are members of Deaf families whose principal language is ASL. The remaining approximate 90 percent of the population are born to hearing families and are consequently potential members of a different cultural group from their own parents. State-operated residential schools for the deaf are the primary places where enculturation of these children takes place (Meadow, 1972: 24). There, through peers from Deaf families and through a Deaf adult staff, if any are present, this process is carried on. This is done informally, often surreptitiously and without the official sanction of the educational establishment. Hence the transmission of culture and language takes place. This is a cultural group whose majority acquires its primary trait—language—not from parents but from peers. For the majority of the population, it is at the residential school where the deaf child begins the process of identification with a Deaf group.

A Brief Cultural History of Deaf America

Herskovits reminds us that "the folklore of a people cannot be understood without an understanding of the culture to which it belongs (1948: 418)." Considering how much of our socialization and education depends on language, we cannot understand the culture of Deaf people without understanding the educational system that controls the Deaf individual's enculturation and linguistic development. To get a true picture of that educational system, we must look at a brief history of its evolution together with the development of American Sign Language.

In 1815 the Rev. Thomas Hopkins Gallaudet, a Protestant minister from Connecticut, traveled to Europe to learn of methods of educating deaf children. In 1817, he returned to the United States with a Deaf Frenchman, Laurent Clerc, and together they established the first permanent school for the deaf in Hartford, Connecticut. This seemingly benign event has much to do with the development of American Sign Language as we see it today. The fact that the American Asylum for the Education of the Deaf and Dumb (now the American School for the Deaf) in Hartford was established as a residential school created a linguistic community of Deaf people communicating in a visual mode. Laurent Clerc had taught French Sign Language (FSL) to Gallaudet, and together they provided linguistic role models for the students.

On this historical basis alone the French were long credited with the establishment of ASL, and ASL was long thought wholly derived from FSL. However, historical linguistic study, principally by James Woodward (1978) and Woodward and Erting (1975), reveals that while approximately 60 percent of today's ASL vocabulary can be traced to FSL cognates, 40 percent cannot. This provides strong evidence that, while the introduction of FSL and the existence of an environment conducive to language development were pivotal in the development of modern day ASL, there was some indigenous form of sign prior to that time.

During the half century following the founding of the Hartford school, other schools for the Deaf were established and administered by hearing educators trained by Clerc—most notably in New York (1818), Pennsylvania (1820), Kentucky (1823), Ohio (1829), Missouri (1838), and Virginia (1839). Later, there were schools founded by Deaf individuals in Arkansas, Florida, Indiana, New Mexico, Oregon and Kansas. By the 1870s more than 40 percent of the teaching staff at the nation's schools for the Deaf were Deaf themselves. These schools and their staff and students provided the linguistic environment within which the language continued to develop. The importance of this creation of the essential environments for the natural development and establishment of a language cannot be overstated. As Stokoe has written, "The foundation of the Deaf subculture resulted essentially from two patterns of behavior: the attendance of deaf children in residential schools and the use of sign language among the students" (1965: 300).

The educational approach that Gallaudet and Clerc used was called the "Combined Method." The children were schooled in the French Sign Language that the two men brought from France, as well as in speech (for further discussion see Lane, 1977: 3-7). In general, this combined oral and manual method was the standard approach in Deaf education until the 1860s when the "Oral Method" took hold.

The Oral Method's emphasis is on speech only. Sign language is forbidden both in and out of the classroom, since proponents of the Oral Method postulate that to allow signing hinders the development of speech in deaf people. They would become lazy. The goal of the Oral Method is to "normalize" deaf children so they can be like hearing people. In fact, a look at old Deaf Education texts reveals references to teaching the child to hear. Children who failed at the Oral Method were often thought to be slow or stupid and were sent as a last resort to a Manual or Combined program. It was this shift to the Oral Method that began what some refer to as "The Hundred Year's War" — The Oral/Manual Controversy. (for further discussion see Lane, 1985, 1992; Winefield, 1987; Mindel & Vernon, 1971; Jacobs, 1989; Brill, 1971).

This shift in educational philosophy occurred at the same time that there was a shift in representation of deaf people in the educational decision-making process. In the mid-1800s there had been an acceptance of Deaf educators in Deaf education. However, as the shift to oralism took hold, this acceptance of Deaf teachers, and of Deaf administrators being involved in the decision-making process, began to wane. In fact, many of the Deaf schools that had been founded by Deaf people gradually were taken over by hearing administrators (Jacobs, 1989). The rise of the Oral Method brought a decline in self-determination for Deaf people and an impingement of their language by decision-makers outside of the Deaf community and Deaf experience.

By 1880, an International Conference of Teachers of the Deaf held in Milan, Italy, resolved to settle the Oral/Manual conflict. They concluded:

> The congress, considering the incontestable superiority of speech over signing in restoring the deaf mute to society, and in giving him a more perfect knowledge of language, declares that the oral method ought to be preferred to that of signs for the education of the deaf and dumb. (Gordon, 1892, xvi)

Notably, there were no Deaf persons involved in drafting the resolution.

With hearing people dominating the decision-making in Deaf education and with the spread of the Oral Method, attempts to suppress ASL were numerous and strong. It was postulated that if deaf children were to sign, it would hamper their development of speech and retard their development of English. This was felt so strongly that deaf children often had their hands struck with a ruler, put in paper bags, tied to their chair or otherwise immobilized as a punishment for even the most simple of gestures. And, those practices were not confined to the nineteenth century. According to one informant, being locked in a dark broom closet was one punishment for signing used in a New York City school as recently as the 1950s. It is amazing that despite all the years of fervent suppression of ASL, the language still remains—widespread and vital.

In response to what it saw as a fearful trend—a kind of linguistic genocide—the National Association of the Deaf in 1913 initiated a film project for the preservation of sign language. In his presentation titled The Preservation of the Sign Language George W. Veditz, the then president of the NAD, stated:

A new race of pharaohs that knew not Joseph are now taking over
the land and many of our American schools. They do not understand
signs for they cannot sign. They proclaim that signs are worthless
and of no help to the deaf. Enemies of the sign language, they are
enemies of the true welfare of the Deaf. We must, with these various
films, protect and pass on our beautiful signs as we now have
them.[2]

The film project continued until 1920 recording some of the
more active bearers of the traditions of Deaf people and those
whose signing was esteemed as the most eloquent.

But oralism continued to be the more dominant philosophy in
the schools, with the manual method reserved primarily for those
who failed at oral means. Although its use was formally discouraged and often punished, ASL continued to be used in the social
confines of the dormitory, on the unsupervised playground and
within the Deaf family. With its long history of overt oppression
the fact that ASL survives today is living testimony to the NAD
film's emphatic closing statement by Veditz, "As long as we have
Deaf people on earth, we will have signs..." The film project ac-
complished its goal of preserving the sign language of the early
20th century. It is sad, but indicative of the times that the films lay
forgotten in the basement of the Gallaudet University Library until their relatively recent discovery and resurrection, for the project
was perhaps the last significant attention ASL received until the
late 1950s.

Although there are an estimated 500,000 present-day native
users in the United States and Canada (ASHA, 1974: 17), the survival of ASL has not been without cost. Many native signers still
have negative, ambivalent feelings about their language and even
associate feelings of guilt with its use. It is not uncommon to find
an informant who will describe their ASL as a "broken form of English" and apologize for it.

While the Oral/Manual struggle continued, changes were
taking place in the Deaf population that intensified the critical nature of this conflict. Medical advances were lessening the incidence of deafness due to childhood disease, while at the same
time ensuring the survival of babies who were deaf due to prema-
turity. The result: a demographic shift in the composition of the

population, with a dramatic increase in prelingually deaf children—those who became deaf before acquiring language and speech. While the Oral Method might help children who had acquired speech and language before the onset of deafness, the incidence of success would not be the same among prelingually deaf children. For the prelingually deaf individual, the learning of spoken English is particularly arduous. It is a task first requiring the conceptualization of a sound system that has never been heard. Lou Fant created an analogy for hearing people for this language learning task. It is as follows:

> Suppose, for example, you were in a sound-proof, glass booth, equipped only with a pad and pencil. Outside the booth is your instructor, who speaks, reads and writes only Japanese. How long would it take for you to learn Japanese? How well would you learn it? (1972: v)

This would be a difficult, if not impossible task for the average hearing person. However, the hearing person is at least beginning the task with a linguistic competence in a first language. This is not the case for most deaf children.

George Orwell went so far as to say that if you control a people's language, you control the people. When a people are dependent exclusively on a visual mode to acquire language, the suppression of a visual form of language is doubly oppressive.

So we can begin to realize how sensitive this historical issue is for a member of the Deaf community, whose identity is inextricably interwoven with ASL and its use. We can only begin to surmise the impact of this conflict on the Deaf individual and better understand the we and they dichotomy of this minority group: we identify with ASL; they with English. If attitudes toward a language are transformed into attitudes about its users, then what have Deaf individuals learned about themselves from educators who do not even recognize ASL as valid?

The Linguistic Community

Perhaps the most important thing to remember about this culture is that it is a bilingual diglossic community. Its members are a linguistic minority functioning within a larger English-speaking society. The continuum ranges from ASL to signed varieties of English with many variations of pidgin and contact varieties in between (Lucas & Valli, 1992; Stokoe, 1970: 27; Woodward, 1973: 39-46), as the following diagram (Figure 1) illustrates:

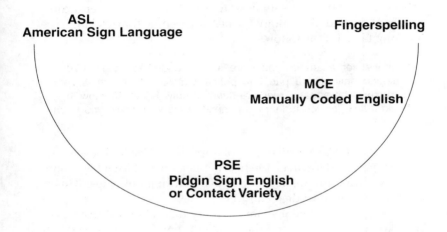

Figure 1
Language and Communication Continuum

FINGERSPELLING: Using 26 hand configurations to form manual representations of the English alphabet, it is used to spell English words manually. It is also used as a borrowing mechanism for ASL of English and other foreign vocabulary.

MANUALLY CODED ENGLISH (MCE): A coded system originally developed to replicate oral language in a manual form, with the idea that if a deaf child could see English the same way a hearing child could hear English, the problem of acquiring a language based in a sound system would be solved for deaf children. It incorporates vocabulary from ASL and adds affixes for -ING, -D, PAST (for irregular verbs), AM, WAS, WERE, IS; uses articles like THE, A; shows plurals with -S; and possessives with -'S; uses pronouns such as

SHE, HE, THEY; and makes use of initialized signs, in which the handshape parameter is changed to correspond with the manual alphabet representation of the first letter of the English word for the lexical item signed. As the name implies, MCE is a parasitic code and not a language.

PIDGIN SIGN ENGLISH (PSE) and CONTACT VARIETIES: A mixture of ASL and English employing, in general, the vocabulary and some structure of ASL in English word order. Certain syntactic markers are fingerspelled; there are no affixes added; uses FINISH for past, and TRUE for all 'to be' verbs; no articles; no plural -S marker, index (POINT) for pronouns. PSE is not a vernacular language of any group, but PSE and other contact varieties, which may be speech supported, are used in contact situations with speakers of English.

AMERICAN SIGN LANGUAGE (ASL): A visual/gestural language, in contrast with English aural/spoken, it is more simultaneous in production than English, which is more sequential. (This is due to the fact that the eye can easily perceive simultaneous bits of information, whereas the ear can only accommodate only one phonological unit at a time.) Object nouns are generally placed first before subject and verb; indexing (POINT) for pronouns; can use FINISH for past. It is the language used by Deaf adults in America today.

We can see some of the distinctions between Fingerspelling, MCE, PSE and ASL in the following glossed sample sentences:

'She bought the car.'

FINGERSPELLING: S-h-e-b-o-u-g-h-t-t-h-e-c-a-r

MCE: SHE BUY + PAST THE CAR

PSE: Point FINISH BUY CAR

ASL: CAR POINT FINISH BUY

'The bus left two hours ago.'

FINGERSPELLING: T-h-e-b-u-s-l-e-f-t-t-w-o-h-o-u-r-s-a-g-o

MCE: THE B-BUS LEAVE + P-PAST 2 H-HOUR + -S P-PAST

PSE: BUS FINISH LEAVE TWO HOUR PAST

ASL: TWO-HOUR PAST BUS FINISH LEAVE

Some members of the signing community may be better skilled in ASL and less so in English or vice versa. And too, some may be balanced in competencies in each language. This situation is perhaps best described by Kannapell in her "Proposed Classification of Deaf Children and Adults" (1974: 9-15) as follows:

ASL Monolinguals They are comfortable expressing themselves only in ASL and understanding ASL.
ASL-Dominant Bilinguals They are comfortable expressing themselves in ASL better than in English and are able to understand ASL better than English (in either printed or signed form).
Balanced Bilinguals They are comfortable expressing themselves in both ASL and English about equally well.
English-Dominant Bilinguals They are comfortable expressing themselves in English and are able to understand English (in printed and signed form) better than ASL.
English Monolinguals They are comfortable expressing themselves only in English (in oral or signed English) and understanding English (in printed or oral or signed English).

It is very much a part of Deaf culture that members must adjust to different situations—dealing with hearing people, with orally trained deaf people and so on. The Deaf person, therefore, functions day-to-day at various points along the diglossic continuum, code-switching to variations unconsciously as the situation demands.

One of the first major works in the sociolinguistic study of ASL was Stokoe's *Sign Language Diglossia* (1969). In this work Stokoe applied the theories of Ferguson (1959) and Fishman (1967) to the use of English and American Sign Language in the American Deaf community and described the bilingual-diglossic situation between English and ASL. He identified the high, or literary, variety as a signed form of English and the low, or colloquial, variety as ASL. He further showed how their use in the Deaf community was parallel to language situations described by Ferguson and Fishman. English is used in formal situations such as the classroom, lecture hall, pulpit, etc., whereas ASL is found in the more informal settings of small groups and intimate conversations. The community generally regards English as superior (if they even consider ASL a language capable of being compared). Some Deaf users of ASL might even argue against the grammatical nature of ASL, stating that it is really a broken form of English or "street language." Within the deaf education system the language taught for the most part is English.

Only relatively recently have published texts for the teaching of ASL come into being. Although some, most notably Baker & Cokely (1980) and Humphries, Padden and O'Rourke (1980), do a remarkable job in describing the language, they are unavoidably limited in that they attempt to represent a visual language in a two-dimensional printed form. To their credit, Baker and Cokely appended video supplements to their work. More recently there is increasing awareness of the need for a video format. A current effort in publishing an ASL text is the *Signing Naturally* Curriculum (Smith, Lentz & Mikos 1988) that has been developed at Berkeley's Vista College. Employing the functional-notional approach to second language learning, video representation of ASL is central to the project.

However, even with these efforts toward creating appropriate curriculums and texts, it is ironic that the formal teaching of ASL to Deaf students is practiced only on a very limited basis. It is only now beginning and most notably only in those schools working on a bilingual/bicultural teaching model, which respects both ASL and English equally.

Perhaps one of the more interesting aspects of the bilingual diglossic situation in the Deaf community, and where it differs from all other examples, is how the two languages are acquired. For less than ten percent of the Deaf community—those who are deaf individuals with Deaf parents—the process of acquiring ASL runs parallel to their hearing contemporaries' acquiring spoken language. The Deaf individual acquires ASL as a first language, informally, in the home setting.

However, for the majority of Deaf individuals—those born to hearing parents—the process is neither predictable nor smooth. For most, the acquisition of ASL will occur in the school setting, principally in the informal setting of the dorm. It will be learned from other children who, most likely, are members of Deaf families. Deaf adults working in this environment will also contribute.

From a diglossic point of view, it is true that these children, like their classmates from Deaf families, are learning ASL in an informal environment and are being taught English in the formal classroom environment. But, on a more psycholinguistic note, they differ in that they are beginning their language acquisition at a much later age—in some cases as late as adolescence—and are generally acquiring language peer to peer instead of adult to child. The exception to this is where the hearing parents are interacting with Deaf adults and are learning ASL early on in their child's development and also serve as linguistic models.

Stokoe points out that the diglossia situation between ASL and English functions like that described by Ferguson and Fishman and that it seems as stable as similar diglossia situations in other cultures.

We see varieties on the English end of the continuum used when community members interact with hearing people. To an extent this shift is made in an effort to communicate with someone more skilled in English and less so in ASL. But this switching to an English-like pidgin or contact variety serves also as a gatekeeping mechanism that keeps hearing outsiders from penetrating and influencing the community (Markowicz and Woodward, 1975; Padden and Markowicz, 1976). As with any minority group, we find that the Deaf community keeps at a safe distance until the outsiders have proven themselves above suspicion. This code-switching not only protects the community from outside influences, but serves also as a mechanism of strengthening the identity and solidarity of the group. The use of ASL for in-group communication serves a separatist function as well as a unifying one.

As Woodward points out,

ASL has served three primary purposes in the deaf community: 1) communication on the interpersonal level, 2) socialization into the deaf culture, and 3) identification of members of the subculture. In all three respects, ASL acts as a powerful cohesive force in the deaf community (1975: 10).

---

[1] The capitalized Deaf will be used in this work to designate the cultural group as opposed to the lower case deaf which will refer to the audiometric condition of not being able to perceive the sounds of speech.

[2] Translation of *The Preservation of Sign Language* is by Carol Padden.

CHAPTER II

FOLKLORE AS A MIRROR OF CULTURE

"Please But" — A Metaphor of Deaf Experience

In the previous chapter, we began to learn about who the Deaf are: their demographics, their customs, their language structure and some of their history both as a community and as an oppressed minority. But these are only objective facts. How do we really find the soul of a people and learn what they as a group are about? Bascom tells us that "amusement is, obviously, one of the functions of folklore, and an important one; but even this statement cannot be accepted today as a complete answer, for it is apparent that beneath a great deal of humor lies a deeper meaning" (1965: 285). The study of the following joke text is based on the belief that through an examination of a community's folklore one can find a reflection of its culture, and it is perhaps through the humor of the group, and its unselfconscious release of anxieties, that one can get closest to the essence of the community. As Dundes aptly puts it, "It is what makes a people laugh that reveals the soul of that people" (1973: 611).

The joke in question has a long history in the American Deaf community. For this collector it has often been the first joke cited when informants are asked for an example of a "Deaf" joke. My discussion is based on 13 texts and informant analyses collected in ASL on videotape. The following is an English translation of one collected text:

> One time a man, well a person, a Deaf person, was driving along
> and stopped at some train tracks because the crossing signal gates
> were down, but there was no train going by. So he waited for a long
> time for a train to go by, but nothing. The person decided then to get
> out of the car and walk to the control booth, where there was a man
> who controlled the railroad gates. He was sitting there talking on the
> phone. The Deaf man wrote in his very best way (elegantly) "Please
> b-u-t" and handed the paper to the controller. The controller looked
> back at the Deaf person quizzically. "Please but? Huh?" He didn't
> understand that.

If you are a nonsigner, you would not find the joke funny at
all. The punch line is a play on sign. There is a substitution of one
of the parameters of ASL, similar to the substitution of a letter in a
spoken word that creates a play on that word.

ASL has four parameters that, together with certain nonman-
ual components (facial expression, body posture, movement of
the head, body and eyes), comprise the phonological system of
that language. Just as in spoken language, the phonology represents the building blocks upon which the language is based.

These parameters of ASL are: 1. hand shape; 2. palm orientation; 3. movement; 4. place of articulation. W e see these illustrated, for example, in the sign for "candy," as illustrated in Figure 2.

1. Hand Shape: /G/, 2. Palm orientation: down, 3. A movement twist (as arrow indicates), 4. Place of articulation: cheek

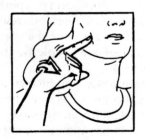

Figure 2

ASL sign CANDY

A change in any one of these parameters can change the meaning of the sign. The signs for "apple" and "jealous" are the same as "candy" except for hand shape as illustrated in Figure 3 (Klima & Bellugi, 11979: 42).

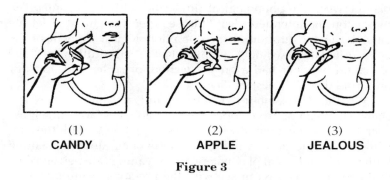

(1)	(2)	(3)
CANDY	**APPLE**	**JEALOUS**

Figure 3

The sign used by the informant for "open the railroad crossing gate" was the /G/ hand shape classifier, as follows. The movement resembles an actual crossing gate being raised and lowered. Note the palm orientation: it is inward, palms facing each other, as in Figure 4.

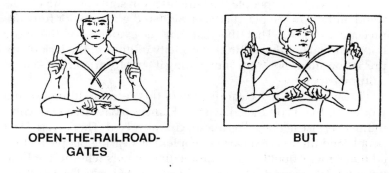

OPEN-THE-RAILROAD-GATES   **BUT**

Figure 4   **Figure 5**

The ASL lexical equivalent for the English word "but" has the same parameters as the above classifier for railroad crossing gate, with the exception of palm orientation, as illustrated in Figure 5—the palms are facing outward.

Thus, the punch line, "Please b-u-t" is an obvious pun-like play between the phonological similarities of the two signs. The play is on the intended idea: "Please, open the gate and let me pass."' The substitution of the one phonological element of the palm orientation would be similar to the substitution in: "The Reverend Spooner had a great affection, or so he said, for 'our queer old dean'" (Koestler 1964: 64),

Whether "Please b-u-t" is a true pun is debatable. There is a change in meaning from "open the railroad gates" to "but," however, the new statement does not make equal sense with the substitution. A true pun would generally evoke a double meaning with the phonological play where both meanings are perceived simultaneously. As we can see with the previous examples, "Our queer old dean" and "Our dear old queen," each statement makes sense. Compare this with the two meanings in the joke: "Please, open the railroad crossing gates' and "Please, b-u-t" The latter does not make equal sense.

The linguistic play is also one step removed. Since the person telling the joke writes the English word b-u-t and does not use the sign "but"' the play is actually on the English gloss.

But even many people who are fluent in sign and who understand and enjoy the play between sign and gloss do not fully appreciate the joke. That this happens is evidence of the more important fact of the cultural specificity of humor: the lack of appreciation stems not from "not getting it" but from a lack of shared cultural experience,

I was witness to a clear display of this cultural difference at a workshop that I conducted at a San Francisco Bay Area Deaf community service agency. The audience was mixed. There were Deaf people and there were hearing people. The hearing people included nonsigners, fluent signers and native signers (children of Deaf parents). We were discussing culture, particularly Deaf culture, and I mentioned that humor was culturally specific. One of the participants asked if I would tell a Deaf joke. I declined, out of lack of comic skills and the feeling that it would be presumptuous for me, a hearing person, to do so, but a Deaf friend—and master co-medienne—consented. I include a translation of her text as one of the variations I collected:

> There is a Deaf man driving along his car. He is hurrying to get home because his wife will get very angry if he is late. He then comes to a railroad crossing and the gates are down. He waits as the train passes. The train is long past and still the gates are down. The man waits and waits and is thinking of how his wife is going to yell if he's late. The Deaf man then gets out of his car and proceeds to the control booth at the crossing, where there is a person who is in charge of all the controls. The Deaf man takes out his pencil and paper and tries to think of the English words to put on the paper requesting that the gates be raised. He thinks and thinks in sign) and says to himself ah ha, and writes the words "Please b-u-t" and hands the paper to the hearing gatekeeper. The gatekeeper does not understand and says, "Huh?"

Of the Deaf and hearing signers who understood the play on the sign, there was a definite qualitative difference in the laughter—a difference that broke along Deaf and hearing lines. The Deaf response was much more intense.

Why the difference, especially since this is a very old joke and many of the Deaf individuals had heard it over and over again? Why funnier to Deaf than to hearing?

Consider again the cultural specificity of humor. The reason that humor is culturally specific for a group is m ore than just language; it is a matter of experience. It becomes clear that the one thing not held in common by the native hearing signers and the Deaf signers is the experience of being Deaf with all its cultural implications. The experience of being a Deaf person in the hearing world is one that is fraught with daily communication frustration, in a way that is generally not a part of a hearing person's life experience. Hearing signers, through professional or familial ties, are generally aware to one degree or another of the frustrations and injustices Deaf people face. However, this awareness is usually on a more cognitive level, not on a deep, affective level.

If we look at the manifest content of the joke we see that the issue is one of communication, or the lack thereof. It is also making fun of Deaf English (for further discussion see Meadow, 1980;

and Charrow, 1975). Like the stilted expression of many whose knowledge of a second language is rudimentary, the language variety referred to as Deaf English is also characterized by simpler structure and overgeneralizations of the grammatical rules of English. For example, if "walk" becomes "walked," why then doesn't "go" become "goed"? If more than one "mouse" is "mice," why is the plural of "house" not "hice"? Another aspect of Deaf English is the substitution of the English gloss for an ASL sign. In the joke, the Deaf person is unable to find the right English words. In this case the right "words" are "Open the railroad gates". Trying his best groping for the right words, the Deaf person falls into using an English gloss of ASL sign, which is identical in all respects but one thus bringing about the punlike play.

Although perhaps not a true pun, the joke does present one frame of reference, "open the railroad crossing gates" and then switches to another, "but" provoking what Koestler terms a bisociative act, as a true pun would. Koestler sees the bisociative act as "the perceiving of a situation or idea...in two self-connected but habitually incompatible frames of reference" (1964: 35). With the connecting of the dissimilar frames of reference an insight into the similarity between the two previously incompatible worlds is revealed. It is this resolution, according to Koestler, that makes us laugh or find something funny. It is my belief that two bisociative acts are at work here: one centering on ASL phonological similarity and the other on the English gloss substitution.

Of the informant analyses that went beyond the description of the play on sign, all referred to the Deaf person's problem with English. To quote a few: "The joke makes fun of Deaf people's English and their problems with writing"; "Deaf people always are having trouble with English"; "English is always a problem, you know that. So its just a way of making fun of it."

One informant went further:

> You have to understand both languages in order to understand the joke. The joke makes fun of the Deaf person. You see Deaf people write down what they say. There are many possible English word choices. The Deaf person in the joke thinks what he wants to say in sign and then ends up writing English gloss. The Deaf person is writing so the hearing person can understand, but really, in sign it is not

funny. The joke makes fun of Deaf English and the writing problems, which "they" blame on the influence of sign language. People blame sign language, so we have jokes that blame sign language. We laugh at that.

"Please b-u-t" is funny as a bilingual play, but again as Bascom asserts, "it is apparent that beneath a great deal of humor lies a deeper meaning" (1965: 285). The deeper meaning here is a crystallized reflection of a historical and sociological experience of the Deaf. It is a picture of lack of control, lack of self-determination, negation of identity, stifled development, blocked communication, external control characterized by benevolent paternalism and authoritarianism, and one of general conflict with the majority culture.

This joke, which has been described as an "old chestnut" by a senior member of the community, is also often referred to as "a joke hearing people wouldn't understand." In *Mother Wit From the Laughing Barrel*, Dundes states that "it is really in the in-group jokes and understanding that a group tests the solidarity of its members. Those who understand are 'with it'; those who do not understand are not 'with it'" (1973: 611). With the explicit statement that a hearing person would not understand the joke, there is an overt definition of in-group/out-group—those who are "with it" and those who are not.

We know from the content of the joke that the gate controller is hearing, as the Deaf man must communicate through written notes. However, frequently in the telling there are embellishments depicting him in a derogatory fashion, talking on and on and occasionally being indifferent to the Deaf man's presence. Just as Basso observes that in Western Apache folkloric tradition the portrayal of "'the Whiteman' serves as a conspicuous vehicle for conceptions that define and characterize what 'the Indian' is not" (1979: j), so we may suggest that the hearing man here serves the same purpose. This is especially true when the hearing man illustrates his indifference to Deaf people and his penchant for speech. In the context of the joke, slurred images of hearing people are safely expressed. The aggression against the majority culture is safely masked by the humor.

Dundes suggests, "Sources of anxiety make the best subjects

for humor" noting that race prejudice is a common theme in Afro-American jokes. (1973: 612). Similarly, "Please b-u-t" focuses on miscommunication and an ambiguous linguistic situation, both of which are daily sources of anxiety within the Deaf community. With often finding one Afro-American group making fun of another, Dundes suggests further that "on the other hand, much humor is entirely intragroup rather than intergroup." (1973: 612). As we have discussed earlier, informant analyses attest to the fact that "Please b-u-t" is also making fun of Deaf people and their misuse of English.

Martineau (1972) suggests that when the in-group humor is disparaging toward an out-group, as in the derogatory depictions of the hearing controller, it may serve to increase morale and solidify the in-group, and/or to introduce and foster a hostile disposition toward the out-group (1972: 116). The former function is certainly fulfilled by this joke, and I would suggest that the latter is also a possible function for some of the tellers of this joke. Martineau also suggests four functions of in-group humor that is disparaging to the in-group: 1. to control in-group behavior; 2. to solidify the in-group; 3. to introduce or foster conflict already present in the group; and 4. to foster demoralization and social disintegration of the group. The latter two do not seem to be as relevant in this situation. Based on my observations and informant analyses, the first two functions do seem to have some validity. The joke-teller displays the proper behavioral norms and attitudes. A common occurrence of Deaf and hearing interaction is dramatized, illustrating sources of mutual anxiety, and this serves to rally the group around a point of solidarity and demonstrate what is "Deaf" and what is not.

Douglas asserts that jokes mirror the incongruity in society. Jokes are anti-structure—an attack on the established order. By joking in a play frame, the resultant disruption challenges the social order on a symbolic level and reaffirms order on a social level (1968: 361),

Further, Feinberg suggests that word play is aggression against conformity, especially, with reference to puns, a rebellion against linguistic conformity. When the language is distorted, it represents a revolt albeit playful, against the rigidity of language (Feinberg 1978: 106). Given the history of linguistic rigidity imposed on the Deaf individual by the majority culture, it is apparent that "Please b-u-t" as a playful linguistic distortion, serves as a particularly satisfying source of rebellion. This is especially true for those who must daily walk the linguistic tightrope between both worlds.

In her paper "The Social Control of Cognition: Some Factors in Joke Perception," Douglas, accepting Freud's analysis that the joke is an attack on control, states, "Since its form consists of a victorious tilting of uncontrol against control, it is an image of the leveling of hierarchy, the triumph of intimacy over formality and unofficial values over official ones" (1968: 365). In the real world, the Deaf community has at least begun to level that hierarchy by identifying what it believes to be the major root of its problems. As one Deaf writer states, "Deaf people have been repressed, restrained and frustrated in their search for an adequate education and equal opportunity for a meaningful life" (Jacobs 1989: 2). The greatest handicap for the Deaf individual is not the inability to hear, Jacobs says, but the ignorance of the hearing world. As he further states, "Many parents and educators fail to realize the critical need for communication" (1989: 12).

"Please b-u-t" symbolically captures the essence of the Deaf situation perfectly: the gates block the way for the Deaf person's own good. It may be reasonable to expect such protection for a while, but the obstruction remains beyond a reasonable time. This parallels what many Deaf individuals experience within the education system.

In control of the situation, of course, is a hearing person, often portrayed talking on the telephone and indifferent to the Deaf person's situation. This is perhaps as close to a Deaf stereotype of a hearing person as we can get.

Frustration mounts as the Deaf person's way continues to be blocked. In some versions, he is expected to arrive home no matter what or his authoritarian wife will be angry. The Deaf person is caught: he has to play the game the hearing way, which for him carries built-in failure, but at the same time he is expected to succeed. This double-bind situation aggravates the frustration and erodes the self-esteem of the individual.

When he gives the hearing gatekeeper the written English note, the gatekeeper does not understand. It should be noted here that speech therapists will often tell deaf children how well they speak. While they may be relatively proficient in the realm of deaf speech, in the outside world it is not uncommon that they will be unable to make their speech understood. The majority culture—the hearing world—does not understand them.

The Deaf person in the joke, as one informant states, "writes his very best" and is still not understood. The slap at hearing control and education is obvious. The Deaf person does his best to communicate as the hearing world has taught him, but communication breaks down. It is, however, a key point, underlining Jacobs' point about an uninformed hearing world, that it is the hearing gatekeeper who fails to grasp the true situation.

The joke serves a second purpose, which sheds light on another source of anxiety. Since this joke is for the bilingual, it may serve as an additional source of group solidarity and identification for those Deaf individuals who have to interact with the hearing world more than their more isolated fellows (who may not have an equal grasp of English). The greater the command of English Deaf individuals have, the more likely they are to be in conflict with themselves.

If "we" use ASL and "they" use English, what happens to the "we" when we use English? Ambivalent feelings about self spring from such situations. The message is that it is not good to be too "hearing." What compounds these ambivalent feelings is that many Deaf people themselves do not recognize that ASL is a real language, having been carefully schooled by the dominant culture to think the contrary. Because Deaf people operate linguistically on a continuum between two languages, using many different varieties as the situation demands (Stokoe 1970: 27; Markowicz and Woodward 1975: 1-15), the possibility exists for greater ambivalence about their own language. Hence, anxiety can crop up when the Deaf attempt to define what they use. Often you will hear an informant say that he signs English or that ASL is really a simplified English. Bilingual play can serve as a mediating factor for the bilingual person who has to function between both languages, mediating the languages and the associated linguistic identity, which is often blurred. By looking at what "we" are and what "we" are not through a vehicle such as "Please b-u-t," a reaffirmation of what "Deaf" is occurs.

"To understand laughter" Bergson tells us, "we must put it back into its natural environment, which is society, and above all we must determine the utility of its function, which is a social one. Laughter" he continues, "must answer to certain requirements of life in common. It must have a social signification" (Bergson 1911: 7). The joke, "Please b-u-t" is still told, is still laughed at and still serves a purpose today for the simple fact that the conflicts still exist. There are anxieties related to communication with the hearing world. There is ambiguity with reference to linguistic identity. The decision-makers in Deaf education are still predominantly hearing and still often paternalistic. The programs for training teachers of the Deaf still for the most part either are based on oral methods or focus on artificial sign systems based on English. Although there has been some improvement, especially with recent moves toward bilingual/bicultural education, the majority culture remains largely uninformed.

Fry states that "a metaphor allows us to treat a psychological phenomenon as a concrete entity and allows us to gather together items of humor, wit, comedy, etc. into one circumscribed object for contemplation" (1963: 35). This joke is a metaphor for the language situation of the community, the experience of the community within the hearing world and the search of the individual for identity. In each of these dimensions, the way is externally blocked. The language is dismissed; the culture is not recognized; and the individual is prevented from gaining true acceptance on any formal level within the hearing world. Thus, the joke reflects the very real conflict that exists between two cultures—hearing and Deaf. At the same time it serves as an aggressive outlet against the majority as well as a vehicle to reaffirm the group identity of the Deaf minority. "Please b-u-t" will continue to be an "old chestnut" as long as the indifference continues and the gates remain down.

CHAPTER III

FOLKLORE AS AMUSEMENT

The Linguistic Creativity of Sign Play

To create a working definition of the term "sign play" I have borrowed from the work of Barbara Kirshenblatt-Gimblett and Joel Sherzer. In their introduction to *Speech Play*—a collection of essays edited by Kirshenblatt-Gimblett—they create their working definition for the term "speech play." With deference to Kirshenblatt-Gimblett and Sherzer, I will take the liberty of applying their concepts and ideas to the context of visual language and coin for this purpose the term "sign play."

Kirshenblatt-Gimblett and Sherzer's first assumption is that each community and culture would have its own definition of what constitutes speech play as it relates to other forms of speech use within the linguistic community.

They further suggest that the idea of

> speech play can be conceived as any local manipulation of elements and relations of language, creative use of a specialized genre, code-variety, and/or style." And, that "it implies a degree of selection and consciousness beyond that of ordinary language use (1976: 1).

They also note the common agreement about play among such scholars as Huizinga, Caillois, Bateson and Sutton-Smith, that it is an activity that is "voluntary, rule-governed and 'carried on for its own sake.'" They acknowledge general agreement, as well, with Huizinga's idea that play "has its aim in itself" (1976: 4).

They continue their description of speech play with the following:

> In a given case, the number of languages made use of may be more than one; the elements and relations manipulated may be of one or of several levels, including the contextual; and the ends served may be various, indeed multiple—comic to be sure, but also religious, artistic, mnemonic, competitive, rehearsal and practice, and, as the term itself implies, sheer play with verbal resources for its own sake (1976: 5).

With the recognition that speech is but a modality for aural language and the modal analogy for visual language is sign, a simple exchange of "sign" for "speech" suffices my purpose here. It is with this resulting definition of "sign" play that this chapter will attempt to examine a traditional verbal art form and offer suggestions toward the meaning of its performance within the American Deaf community.

Employing an interplay between the community's two languages, ASL and English, the ABC Story is a form of linguistic play, carried on for its own sake, that consciously manipulates the phonetic system of one language with the phonological system of the other. Briefly, the mechanism of interplay between English and ASL in the ABC Story is that a story is performed in ASL with the external structure of the English alphabet determining the handshapes used for the story.

Since the American Deaf community is a bilingual diglossic community, with its language continuum ranging between ASL and English, it is to be expected that we would find elements of both languages at play in the folklore of this group.

While there are traditional texts, such as "The Haunted House" or "The Car Race," illustrated herein, the focus of this discussion will be on the form as a genre in itself. The degree of variation in the texts on traditional themes found during collecting suggests that it is the handshape patterning, the linguistic play and performance that are the more salient folkloristic elements. As with much folklore, content may vary widely, but the form remains constant. This interplay of handshapes from the manual

American English alphabet and elements of the phonological system of ASL cuts across genres and is used in various contexts for a variety of purposes. It is employed as a vehicle for performance, as a game, for the telling of adolescent obscene stories, as well as for the teaching of lessons.

Rather than elaborate on the mechanism here in a vacuum, it may prove helpful to examine a text first. A commonly found ABC Story is "The Haunted House."

THE HAUNTED HOUSE

English Synopsis:
A man knocks on the door and slowly the door opens. Warily, he enters the house, his eyes searching the room. Suddenly he hears something fearful. It's a scream—eeek! His eyes glance to see someone running off. The man begins to imagine some very fearful things and decides he'd better hurry along. He then notices the artwork on the wall. It is a picture of a man smoking a cigar. He hears a sound: m-m-m-m-m. Moving closer to the painting, he sees a hole in it. Peeking through the hole, he sees a dead person hanging from the ceiling by a rope. It is the queen. She has hung herself. Suddenly, glancing to the right, the man notices a person standing there. The man is startled as the person is beginning to put a curse on him. With his legs trembling, he holds up a cross to stop the curse and escapes by hastily running off.

Manual Alphabet	ASL Sign	ASL GLOSS (ALL CAPS) AND STORYLINE
		A KNOCK ON THE DOOR
		The DOOR OPENS
		LOOKING AROUND
		HEAR SOMETHING
		E-E-E-K!

Manual Alphabet	**ASL Sign**	**ASL GLOSS (ALL CAPS) AND STORYLINE**

  LOOKING AROUND the room

  He sees someone ZOOM OFF

  He decides he better HURRY ALONG

  He begins to IMAGINE fearfully

  He notices the ART on the WALL

Manual Alphabet	**ASL Sign**	**ASL GLOSS (ALL CAPS) AND STORYLINE**
		It is a picture of a man SMOKING a cigar
		The PICTURE IS ON THE WALL
		The man hears a sound M-M-M-M-M
		He LOOKS AT the painting again
		He notices a HOLE (denoted by an 'O' handshape) in the painting
		There is a dead PERSON SWINGING IN THE AIR

Manual Alphabet	**ASL Sign**	**ASL GLOSS (ALL CAPS) AND STORYLINE**
Q		It is the QUEEN
R		Hanging by a ROPE FROM THE CEILING
S		She has HUNG herself
T		SUDDENLY
U		GLANCING TO THE RIGHT

Manual Alphabet	ASL Sign	ASL GLOSS (ALL CAPS) AND STORYLINE
V		A PERSON STANDING there
W		The person PLACING A CURSE ON THE MAN
X		The man's LEGS ARE SHAKING
Y		He orders the person to STAY where he is
Z		He holds up a cross (repeating 'X') and ESCAPES

What is happening is a play between like images: linguistically, the manual representation of the alphabet of one language, in this case English, and phonological units of another—ASL.

For sign language, the equivalent representation of the English alphabet is called the manual alphabet. Fingerspelling is a coded, letter-by-letter representation of the manual alphabet. An adjunct to ASL, fingerspelling is used for the lexical borrowing from English (for further discussion see Battison, 1978), for proper names, communicating in English and as a means of teaching oral language.

As was discussed in Chapter II the phonology of ASL consists of four parameters, which, in conjunction with certain facial expressions and head and body movements, are analogous to consonant/vowel pattern in spoken language. To reiterate, the four parameters are: 1) handshape configuration; 2) palm orientation; 3) movement; 4) place of articulation. For purposes of this examination of the ABC Story, the parameter we are primarily concerned with is the handshape configuration.

When we compare the manual alphabet chart (Figure 6) with the handshape configuration (Figure 7) on the following page, we can see the corresponding handshapes that interplay in the ABC stories.

Figure 6
Manual Alphabet Chart

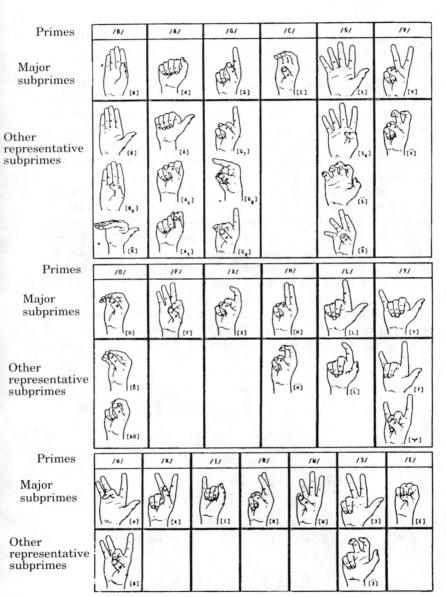

Figure 7
ASL Handshape Configurations

In the mechanism of the form, as the text shows, the English alphabet becomes the external structure for the story. This is similar to jumprope games like "A: My Name is Alice," in which the sequence of the alphabet determines the order of the game. Following alphabetic sequence, as dictated by the form, the storyteller must select a sign with the same hand configuration as each successive letter representation from the manual alphabet. In the opening of "The Haunted House," the handshape for the manual alphabet letter A matches the dominant hand in the sign for a knock on the door, as illustrated in Figure 8.

Manual Alphabet	**ASL Sign**	**ASL GLOSS (ALL CAPS) AND STORYLINE**
		A KNOCK ON THE DOOR

Figure 8
First Handshape in
"The Haunted House"

Because some of the letters of the manual alphabet can be represented by more than one hand configuration—any of which would be considered acceptable—there is a certain flexibility in the selection of matching handshapes. This, then, permits a great deal of creative license in the performance of an ABC story. But it is license within limits. The accepted handshapes for a particular letter, of course, share a similarity of form. For example, B need not be restricted to the major subprime B: a B, Bb or B will serve equally well. What would be acceptably used for each letter of the alphabet is illustrated in Figure 9 (compare with the handshape primes illustrated in Figure 7). Additionally, this collector notes a frequent interchanging among N, H, U and V—all two-finger handshapes—and between M and W, which are three-finger handshapes. As illustrated in Figures 7 and 9, M, N and Q do not have direct equivalents in ASL hand configurations. If a performer is to miss or forget a part of an ABC story, it is often at these points, at which an unfamiliar stretch has to be made.

ASL Handshape	Acceptable Handshapes			
A	A, $\dot{A}$			
B	B, B, B_b, $\hat{B}$			
C	C			
D	G_d			
E	E			
F	F			
G	G, G_1, G_g			
H	H, $\overset{...}{H}$			
I	I			
J	I			
L	L, $\overset{...}{L}$			
M	W			
N	$\overset{...}{H}$			
O	O, $\hat{O}$, $_bO$			
P	K			
Q	G_g, G			
R	R			
S	A_s			
T	A_t			
U	H, $\overset{...}{H}$			
V	V, V			
W	W			
X	X			
Y	Y, $\dot{Y}$, ⊔			
Z	G_1, G			

Figure 9
Acceptable Handshapes

Now that we have a sense of both the limits and the flexibility of the form, we can examine another text and see the interaction between sign and external structure.

THE CAR RACE

English Synopsis:

The cars are low and sleek racing cars. Spectators are astonished as they watch them speed past. The winning driver turns out to have a swelled head and, looking at another driver, says, "I beat you." The second driver is jealous and thinks to himself: "Boy, is he big-headed. He thinks he's king of the road." The second driver reflects on what had happened before and why he did not win the race. He remembers starting the car. With hands on the steering wheel, he was ready to go. He looked at the dash gauges and noticed that something was wrong with the car. He was worried that it would not be safe and decided to put his racing plans in abeyance and not enter the race. Therefore, he did not win the race because he was not able to compete.

| **Manual Alphabet** | **ASL Sign** | **ASL GLOSS (ALL CAPS) AND STORYLINE** |

COMPETITION.
It's a Race.

There are
LOW SLEEK
RACING CARS
speeding around

Their WHEELS
are vibrating

The STICK SHIFT
is vibrating

Manual Alphabet	**ASL Sign**	**ASL GLOSS (ALL CAPS) AND STORYLINE**
		EEEEEEEK the wheels screech
		Spectator's EYES watch the cars
		The cars GO/ZOOM past
		The winning driver turns to another race driver and says "I BEAT YOU!"
		I-I-I, he displays a very large ego

Manual Alphabet	**ASL Sign**	**ASL GLOSS (ALL CAPS) AND STORYLINE**

The second driver is
JEALOUS

and says "Boy he thinks he's KING of the road."

"What a SWELLED HEAD!"

"M" (missing from text)

The second driver
LOOKED BACK
to what had happened
to him and why the
other driver had won

Manual Alphabet	ASL Sign	ASL GLOSS (ALL CAPS) AND STORYLINE
		"O" (missing from text)
		"P" (missing from text)
		He put the KEY in the ignition and started the car
		READY to go
		Hands on the steering wheel (Both "S" and "T" represented by "A_s" and "A_t" respectively, are used in succession

Manual Alphabet	ASL Sign	ASL GLOSS (ALL CAPS) AND STORYLINE
U		He LOOKS AT the dash gauges
V		He's STUCK. Something is wrong with the car.
W		WORRY (signed with "W" handshape
X		His racing plans are HELD IN ABEYANCE
Y		WHY didn't he win? Because he couldn't enter the race
Z		The informant signed "Z" while shaking head in negative fashion — meaning too bad, but couldn't go.

"The Car Race" is a commonly elicited ABC story. Informants who themselves could not perform ABC stories often would refer to having seen them and would almost invariably cite "The Car Race" as an example. Many would attempt it but usually could not remember past the letter E in the story.

"The Car Race" appears to be a traditional text. Elicitations often begin with little variation. However, when the storyteller gets to the middle of the story, considerable variation occurs. For example, another text that begins the same way concludes with an in-depth character sketch of a suave race car driver who thinks quite a lot of himself. Other variations on this and other traditional texts exist, but the performance of the form appears to be more important than the content.

Although the content of the ABC Story is not the prime focus of the performance, there are contexts in which the content is of importance. In some cases the strict form allows the performance of taboo content. One example of this is the use of the ABC Story at an adolescent slumber party or gathering. On such occasions the external structure provides a safe device for explorations of vocabulary and subject matter that might otherwise be difficult to discuss openly. The following version of "The Haunted House" (cited earlier) was titled "The Mystery Story" by the informant.

THE MYSTERY STORY

English Synopsis:

A man knocks (A) on a door (B) and the door opens slowly. He enters and begins to search (C) the house because he had heard screams (E). His eyes (F) search the room and suddenly he sees a body (G) of a woman lying (H) exhausted on the floor. He then imagines (I) what had happened before—a frenzied scene of two people engaged in a sexual marathon (J-Z)..

The typical slumber party was described by this informant as being composed of perhaps six to ten Deaf high school girls 16 to 18 years old. Activities included discussions of clothes and boys; "lying" about sex (i.e., "I've never done that!"); and going out to try to meet boys. The fact that "The Mystery Story" version we see here is a variant of the traditional "Haunted House" text, and that it comes to no conclusive point (the traditional "Haunted House" texts have a more complete storyline), suggests that it serves a purpose other than the elicitation of a story. In this case it appears to be used primarily as a vehicle for the exploration of "forbidden" and "mysterious" territory, i.e., sexual activity.

In another context, a male informant from the Pennsylvania School for the Deaf (now a California resident) remembered that when he was a young adolescent, ABC stories were used as a vehicle to show off "street smarts," which he and his classmates would learn outside of the residential school while on vacations. The creation of these ABC stories were a way of nonchalantly demonstrating some newfound ways-of-the-world. Such worldly activities might include anything from stealing hub caps to sexual explorations.

The ABC Story is evident in other contexts. One hearing informant related that his Deaf mother would use ABC stories as a bedtime amusement for him. According to the informant, she did this to teach him the English alphabet. He was unable to remember specific texts but said that they were often about animals and that they varied with the exception of the ending. The Z was always Z-Z-Z-Z-Z-Z, indicating it was time to sleep.

We find the performance of ABC stories such as "The Car Race" and "The Haunted House" generally at the gathering of an all Deaf group. One informant said that such stories "would never be done in public, just within the group." This stands to reason since to appreciate the stories a viewer would have to have an understanding of ASL; however, hearing signers who would have the ability to understand the language and appreciate the performance do not, as a rule, participate in the creation of ABC stories, nor do they tend to perform them. The creation of ABC stories appears to be an activity of the Deaf community and not of the larger signing community, which is both hearing and Deaf.

When asked to pinpoint when they first encountered ABC stories or when they themselves began creating them, the majority of informants responded that they first came upon or participated in this activity as adolescents and young adults.

Most learned the form from older peers. One informant recalled first seeing them when he was a junior high school student at Pennsylvania School for the Deaf, and a visiting college student from Gallaudet performed some. Another learned them from a fellow student in junior high who was a couple of years older. "We were just hanging around on the porch one Saturday afternoon and we began playing with the idea after we saw one." Still another learned them first from his Deaf father, who thought his son would find them amusing.

Since, as we discussed earlier, cultural transmission in the Deaf community, occurs more from peer to peer than from parent to child, it is not unusual that we find the majority of informants learning the form from slightly older peers. Of course, with the preponderance of ABC stories being first learned in adolescence their peer-to-peer transmission is not unusual: adolescence is a time when there is more focus on peer-to-peer interaction. Culture in general—is transmitted peer to peer. The use of ABC Stories does not stop with adolescents; however, it is perhaps young adults who polish and perfect their performance. There are incidences of performance by older adults, too, such as those parents who teach them to their children, as mentioned earlier. Also, there are refined theatrical performances of ABC stories included in Deaf variety shows. One example is Gilbert Eastman's[3] performance of "Theatre" at *Celebration: Deaf Artists and Performers* held at the University of California, Berkeley, in May 1982. "Theatre" is a compendium of four ABC stories depicting different aspects of theatre—costuming, performing, audience appreciation, etc.—with each aspect performed A-Z.

We don't find many older adults playing with ABC stories, except for those found in group storytelling games at a party. Those who do perform ABC stories do so because they have acquired a reputation for expertise. The community considers their performances to be the epitome of the form. When discussing the requisites for attaining a degree of skill and reputation for performance, informants generally agreed that a high degree of competence in ASL was necessary, with the very best performers—whether young or old—possessing a strong Deaf identity.

An excellent example of transmission of an ABC story is found in "The Class Reunion." This appears to be a recent text originally created by a young woman from eastern Canada. A similar version was performed as an example of an ABC story at Celebration '82 in Berkeley. The performer (a New Jersey native and then California resident) collaborated with another Deaf individual who had seen "The Class Reunion" performed in the East. The person who had seen it performed thought the Celebration version was not exactly like the original, but thought it was a good story. It was performed by someone who has a reputation for storytelling and a very strong Deaf identity. It was very well received by the Deaf and sign-skilled audience.

THE CLASS REUNION

English Synopsis:

This is a characterization of the storyteller at his class reunion. It opens with a greeting of one person: "Hello, how are you doing?"—and shaking the person's hand. Then turning to yet another individual, he says, "You, Esther! (looking her over) You're so thin!" Turning to another person, he says, "Hi, Joan!" (Nodding his head acknowledging her, he then notices she is smoking.) "You're smoking, I'm surprised at you!" Someone nudges him on the shoulder; "Dumb me, I didn't realize it was her. She looks so old.") Shifting to another person, he says, "Ted! We can certainly look back at all the memories." Returning to his own thoughts, he thinks, "Wow! It's really something. There are so many old friends now coming together here, to this place."

Manual Alphabet	**ASL Sign**	**ASL GLOSS (ALL CAPS) AND STORYLINE**
A		YOURSELF (This, coupled with the following sign, can be interpreted as "Hello, how are you doing?")
B		HELLO
C		(gesture of shaking hands with 'C' handshape)
D		YOU!
E		ESTER (a name sign[4])

Manual Alphabet	**ASL Sign**	**ASL GLOSS (ALL CAPS) AND STORYLINE**

LOOKING HER OVER

You're so THIN

(Turning to another person)
HI!
(This is a fingerspelled
loan sign)

JOAN (a name sign)
(head nodding to
acknowledge her)

You're SMOKING!
(with slight look of
disgust)

| **Manual Alphabet** | **ASL Sign** | **ASL GLOSS (ALL CAPS) AND STORYLINE** |

I'm SURPRISED at you!

Someone nudging the storyteller's shoulder with an 'M' handshape

NO! Oh no! It's…
('NO is a fingerspelled loan word incorporating 'N' and 'O' handshapes)

PAT (an name sign)

The 'Q' handshape with fingertips touching forehead (vertically, then horizontally) depicting a small block as in 'blockhead'. This can be glossed as OH! DUMB ME! I didn't

Manual Alphabet	**ASL Sign**	**ASL GLOSS (ALL CAPS) AND STORYLINE**
R		REALIZE that she was so
S		OLD
T		(shift to new person) TED (a name sign)
U		(reminiscing together) We can certainly LOOK BACK at all the memories.
V		LOOKING BACK (also signed with a 'V' handshape)

Manual Alphabet	**ASL Sign**	**ASL GLOSS (ALL CAPS) AND STORYLINE**
W		WOW! It is really something.
X		There are so many old FRIENDS
Y		NOW
Z		(With the movement of the handshape 'Z' elements of these two signs are used to convey COMING-TOGETHER-HERE-TO-THIS-PLACE

The audience at *Celebration '82* consisted of approximately equal numbers of Deaf and hearing members, most of whom were sign-skilled. The audience's response to this performance was one of extra delight: first, for the particularly adroit performance; and second, for seeing new material. It was particularly well received by the hearing members. Most of the time hearing signers appreciate the play between the alphabet and ASL in ABC stories and are generally amused. However, their response is still qualitatively different—more detached—from that of a Deaf audience. Since the hearing response to "The Class Reunion" was more enthusiastic than usual, it suggests that it was the content—a situation with which both audiences identified—that crossed the invisible barrier between the two worlds.

This ABC story has many instances of conventional uses of fingerspelling in ASL. One example is the use of name signs, which usually involve the first letter of the person's name signed either on the body or in some neutral space. (For further discussion of name signs see Chapter 5). Another example is in the use of fingerspelled loan words such as #HI and #NO. These are instances of English words that have been borrowed into ASL through fingerspelling and are now lexical items in their own right, not merely the fingerspelling equivalent of the words.

This ABC story also incorporates a nonlexical behavior in the performance—the "shoulder nudge." This is a cultural behavior for gaining a person's attention. It is interesting that these instances occur most often where the ASL counterpart of the manual alphabet handshape is either little used in ASL, i.e., E, J, P, T, or not a part of ASL phonology, i.e., M.

The "Class Reunion" story had the highest number of such instances in my entire sample of ABC stories. It was also the only story in the sample that was created in rather short order and was specifically for public performance.

Often informants referred to ABC stories as something one would create and perfect to perform at a social gathering in order to show off one's ability at being able to create a story with built-in restrictions on handshape. More than once it was noted that someone needed a measure of cleverness to make it all the way to Z. One informant said, "It's a knack—some can do it, some can't." More important is the attitude toward one who has the "knack."

They are often sought out and coaxed again and again to perform.

If we look beyond individual performance for small groups, we find that the ABC Story has been recently incorporated into theatrical productions of sign art, such as at Celebration mentioned earlier and in the Fairmont Theatre of the Deaf in Cleveland, Ohio. In the latter, a production of their original creation entitled "Circus of Sign" highlighted the performance of traditional pieces such as the *ABC Story*. Concurrent with the comparatively recent burst of pride in Deaf heritage, we see an increased incorporation of traditional "Deaf" identified material within public performance.

The variation in contexts where we find ABC stories as well as cross-genre applications such as word or iconic representations, which will be discussed next, seems to give greater credence to the idea that, while traditional texts do exist for some ABC stories, it is the form that is the primary folkloristic element that is passed from generation to generation.

ABC Texture in Other Forms

Two apparently newer but related forms of sign play employing this same mechanism of external English-based structure and ASL-performed content are what could be called Fingerspelled/ASL Word Characterizations and Fingerspelled/Iconic Representations. Again, these titles are my creation and are offered solely for purposes of description and discussion. They do not necessarily represent what they are called within the community. Terms such as "fingerspelling mime," "fingerplay" and "handshape patterning" or "ASL words" are in relatively common use, and often refer to both forms.

Fingerspelled/ASL Word Characterizations

Fingerspelled / ASL Word Characterizations follow the same form as the ABC Story—the handshape configurations of ASL are linked with the handshape of the manual alphabet. However, the letter sequence—rather than being the alphabet—spells out a word or words. The content of the characterization is usually a dramatization in ASL that illustrates some aspect of the word. One example is "Baby," which follows.

HANDSHAPES	ASL SIGNS	CONTENT

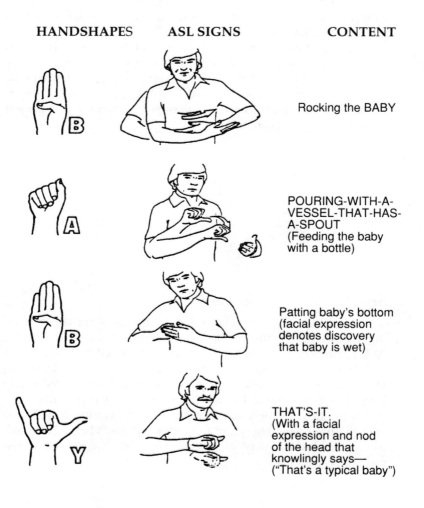

Rocking the BABY

POURING-WITH-A-VESSEL-THAT-HAS-A-SPOUT
(Feeding the baby with a bottle)

Patting baby's bottom
(facial expression denotes discovery that baby is wet)

THAT'S-IT.
(With a facial expression and nod of the head that knowlingly says—
("That's a typical baby")

The entire performance consists of ASL signs blended with mimed expression to give us a vignette of "Baby"—rocking, caring, feeding, patting and the "typical" always seeming wet. The informant for this example, who teaches deaf children, said he uses this technique in teaching his students the meaning of English words. An actor, formerly with the National Theatre of the Deaf, he is particularly skilled at this form of linguistic play.

Thus far in my collecting, it appears that this form requires a higher degree of competency in both languages than that needed for the ABC stories. Further, it and the Iconic Representation appear to be relatively new forms. Most elicitations were from younger members of the Deaf community—20 to 40 years old— and examples seem to date back only to the 1960s. Some older informants had never seen the form before but were delighted at seeing an example.

Another example of this technique is "Golf," an example of which is performed by Alan Barwiolek on the *American Culture: the Deaf Perspective Deaf Folklore* videotape (San Francisco Public Library, 1984).

GOLF

ASL Handshapes   **Contents**

GOLF TEE
Left hand - 'G'
handshape palm up

GOLF BALL
Right hand - 'O'
handshape sets
on tee

GOLF CLUB
Left hand - 'L'
swings and hits
GOLF BALL

BALL FLYING
Right hand - 'F'
handshape flies
in the air

Some of my informants are current or former members of the National Theatre of the Deaf (NTD). Several of them mentioned that they would create these sign-plays to amuse themselves during the long hours spent traveling by bus on their national tours. It appears that NTD has served as a mechanism of transmission for these Fingerspelled/ASL Word Characterizations, especially when the company tours as the Little Theatre of the Deaf, performing at the nation's schools for the deaf.

Another informant tells of his creation of a Fingerspelled/ASL Word Characterization while en route from his native state of Washington to Southern California, where he was to begin college at age 19. The text follows:

HANDSHAPES	**ASL SIGNS**	**CONTENT**
		SEARCHING for a
	 	GIRL of a particular SHAPE
		'L' handshapes form a picture frame for sizing up
		SLENDER would be
		PERFECT

HANDSHAPES	ASL SIGNS	CONTENT
O		NONE around
R		I'm READY to
N		find and RECRUIT a girl
I		Others would have to IMAGINE what I would do
A		That would be for me to know — my SECRET. It's my business.

This characterization is not what one would commonly see depicting the meaning of California: images of gold, redwoods or hot tubs. However, it is obvious that this is a perfect illustration of the meaning of California for this performer at the time. The content is more important here than in the ABC Story. "California" may have been created for his own amusement, but the content clearly reflects what was on the mind of this 19-year-old moving to a new state, to attend a new school, and subsequently to begin a new social life.

Fingerspelled/Iconic Representation
Another recent and closely related form of this folk genre is the Fingerspelled/Iconic Representation. Like the ASL Word Characterization, it follows the external structure of the letter sequence of a word or words to dictate the sequence of handshapes. However, rather than being a linguistic dramatization of the word's meaning, the Fingerspelled/Iconic Representation delivers a visual portrayal of the word itself. For example:

"FALLING LEAF"
Figure 10

Watching Dorothy Miles, a Deaf actress, perform this with the NTD in a play called *My Third Eye*, one could imagine a leaf falling effortlessly through the air in a twisting and turning fashion, then lighting gently on the ground.

Another example of this form, also performed by Dorothy Miles, is "Bouncing Ball," as illustrated in Figure 11. The words are spelled out while the hand portrays the image of a ball bouncing.

These iconic representations of meaning approach being visual analogs of onomatopoeia. This concept is demonstrated particularly well in "Reflection," illustrated in Figure 12. The left hand mirrors the right, as a pool of water would. Together they spell out r-e-f-l-e-c-t-i-o-n, as they move across the surface of the pool.

These two newer forms—the *Fingerspelled/ASL Word Characterization* and the *Fingerspelled/Iconic Representation*—have an important added factor not found in the more general ABC stories. They not only interplay elements of the two languages but play with the sense of them as well. As mentioned before, many examples of these forms were elicited from younger members of the Deaf community, especially professional performers. These informants have a great command of both languages. Moreover, those who are actors are frequently involved in translation of works written in English to ASL. It is to be expected that such members of the community would be able to stretch the boundaries of a folk form. However, it is the general form itself—the interplay between sign and an external structure in the ABC Story—that is rooted in the long history of the Deaf community.

Figure 11
"BOUNCING BALL"

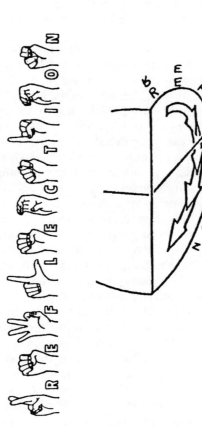

Figure 12
"REFLECTION"

The structure of the ABC Story—in which the external ordering is determined by the English alphabet, but the internal expression is performed in ASL—is, in a sense, a metaphor for the language situation in which the community functions. The external rules and order are determined by the English-speaking, hearing world with the internal communication performed among Deaf people in ASL. Thus, this display of the ABC structure divides that which is English (hearing) and that which is ASL (Deaf) and defines the group.

With the formal educational establishment historically all but ignoring the existence of ASL, the distinction between the languages and their use on a cognitive level is not clear. The misconception that ASL is a basic form of English "on the hands" is one held not only by much of the hearing world, but by many Deaf people themselves. For those Deaf people, ASL is broken English or "street talk." To be a success, to be literate, one must be skilled in English. To have competency in or to learn a language is synonymous with having competency in or learning English—language means English. Yet on the affective level, the use of ASL is very clearly that which identifies you as being Deaf.

As one might imagine, this situation produces a great amount of ambivalence with reference to language and attendant identity. A function served by the ABC Story may be the reconciliation of this English/ASL ambivalence in language and identity for both the Deaf individual and the Deaf community in general.

With the majority world offering a confused picture for linguistic and cultural identity, the play frame of the ABC Story offers performer and audience alike a safe arena for linguistic exploration and expression. The idea that "this is play" is expressed in the performance style and posture of the performer. The play between ASL and English alphabet enables the player and audience to contrast the use of each. As Garvey states, "...the very idea of play depends on contrast (1977: 5)." The English/ASL linguistic play reveals a paradox of sorts. With the formal educational institutions having labeled English a "real" language and ASL an "unreal" language, it appears that the sign play of the ABC Story attempts to reconcile this paradox and reverse the perception of ASL, elevating it to a "real" language.

The bilingual Deaf adult functions daily within the English/

ASL paradox. The English/ASL contrast that is established in the ABC Story implicitly carries the notion not only of separateness but of equalness as well.

Beyond the assertion that ASL is real, the very performance of creative expression within the language (as illustrated in the play with the English/ASL contrast) establishes ASL as real. The deliberate, playful manipulation of ASL in the ABC Story reflects the performer's intuitive awareness of linguistic form (Klima and Bellugi, 1978: 339). One must have something that is real and know what it is before one can play with it.

On another level, the ABC Story can serve to mediate or integrate the two worlds within which the Deaf individual functions. As discussed earlier, most Deaf individuals are bilinguals in varying degrees, some stronger in one language than the other, and some with balanced competencies in both. The ABC Story can define that situation as well as integrate elements of both languages. Thus, the process facilitates the practical integration of the two worlds. This is especially true, I believe, with ABC sign play as found in Fingerspelled/ASL Word Characterizations. In this form, the play is with the sense of the word spelled in English. The play is beyond the phonological level alone, it is morphological as well. This sort of play would be of particular benefit for the bilingual person who is in the position of constantly translating meaning from one language to another—from one culture to another.

It is interesting to note that the Fingerspelled/ASL Word Characterizations seem to be a relatively recent form. This form of ABC play appears to have begun in the 1960s—a time when there began to be a higher incidence of Deaf people interacting with the hearing world. The National Theatre of the Deaf began its tours, and the movement accelerated toward civil rights for disabled people and communication access for deaf people. There was also the beginning of a more general acceptance of Deaf people, with sign language classes coming out of the church basement and into the classroom of mainstream America. These events coincided with the beginnings of the Total Communication movement within deaf education.

Total Communication is a philosophy that includes the use of sign language in the education of children. Thus, we see this form of sign play emerging at the same time that Deaf and hearing worlds were in the process of integrating to a greater degree. One cannot assert that one caused the other. However, it is a tidy fit in terms of the emergence of a folk form and the reality of the social situation at the time.

Another function of ABC play that cannot be overlooked is its role in increasing linguistic competence. The repetitiousness of play activity leads to mastery of the materials played with. From an educational point of view, play enhances competency. Word and sign games are often an integral part of Deaf social functions. This is similar to the Thai children's bilingual play studies by Mary Haas (1964: 301-304), in which play between Thai and English translations functioned to increase the children's proficiency in both languages. The sign play within the ABC Story, especially when used as a game, furthers the development of language skills for the Deaf individual.

The storytelling within the ABC play occurs in ASL. The successful performer must be highly skilled in the language, have a strong Deaf identity and, as one person suggested, in essence be the epitome of Deafness. Several informants identified the ABC Story as "truly Deaf" or "really Deaf." Thus, performance of an ABC Story is Deaf performance and, as such, is lauded by the Deaf audience.

The sign play of the ABC Story can be seen as a mediation between the two poles of linguistic identity—external English control and internal ASL affective expression, simultaneously. Although there are many possible and simultaneous functions that the ABC Story may serve for this folk group, on a symbolic level it very closely parallels the linguistic situation Deaf people experience in this country. Like the alphabet, which is learned by rote and does not deviate, the hearing order is regimented A-Z. The Deaf person is expected to perform by the dictates of the external, well-ordered rules and yet, in clear juxtaposition within that frame, the spirit, soul, art and identity are expressed in ASL.

---

[3] Gilbert Eastman is Professor of Dramatic Art at Gallaudet University; a director, an actor; and founding member of the National Theatre of the Deaf.

[4] Names of people are generally fingerspelled. However, often Deaf

people will use a name sign. Name signs are a convention within the Deaf Community, which usually involves the first initial of the person's name being signed somewhere on the body or in neutral space in front of the signer. A name sign can incorporate distinguishing physical or personality characteristics of the individual such as an initial handshape signed on the head denoting intelligence. The English given names appearing in this text are of my creation, since they were elicited only as name signs. This is for illustrative purposes only.

CHAPTER IV

THE EDUCATIVE FUNCTION OF FOLKLORE

The Traditional Group Narrative of Deaf Children

> When we were children trying to develop language meaningful to us, we invented many stories like this.
> —*My Third Eye*,[5] National Theatre of the Deaf (1971)

Folk traditions exist within any identifiable cultural group. These traditions, passed from generation to generation, survive for one basic reason: they continue to serve vital functions for the group. Among others, they help to define the culture and maintain the group's sense of identity. Perhaps most important for the purposes of this chapter, they serve as an educating tool for the learning of cultural rules, values and specific competencies. This is as true for the culture of Deaf people as for any other.

This chapter will first briefly look at the role that folk traditions play within a culture and then more closely examine a folk tradition that is widespread in the folk group of Deaf children: the group narrative.[6] This examination is based on collection of group narratives in context at the California School for the Deaf at Berkeley (now at Fremont); in-studio video recording of storytelling sessions and interviews of Deaf children, age eight to ten; a recorded performance by the National Theater of the Deaf of an example of the genre (which is publicly available); and interviews with Deaf adults reflecting on their childhood experiences at various state schools for the Deaf, among them New Jersey, Oregon, California (Berkeley and Riverside), Kansas, Ohio and Washington state. We will also examine other materials within the folk tradition that contribute to the development of narrative competency.

Beyond this inquiry, this chapter will explore the benefits of using traditional folk material such as the group narrative in the formal education of Deaf children. We will examine how the spontaneous folk play in group narrative provides an environment for two complementary phenomena: the learning of language in a social context and the development of social competence in a linguistic context. And how Deaf customs, games and storytelling arts lend to the development of narrative competencies in Deaf children.

FOLKLORE

It is unfortunate that popular usage of the term "folklore" often implies something that is not true, or is wrong or refers to traditions that are old and dying out. On the contrary, folklore is alive and well and continues to serve the needs and desires of the folk group.

Much of a person's enculturation in this world occurs through folklore. It is such a close and integral part of our lives that we take it as much for granted as the air we breathe. Its functions in our lives are many: It amuses us; it validates our culture, reaffirms our identity, and serves to maintain conformity to accepted patterns of behavior (Bascom, 1965: 279-298). Folklore also educates us; through its various forms we gain knowledge in different areas. Through myth we learn of our relationship with nature and the supernatural. Through legend we learn of how things got to be the way they are. This can also provide us with a sense of history—a sense that things evolve and that the past connects to the present and to ourselves. Through family stories and first-person reminiscences we also learn of our heritage, our heroes and those we desire to emulate.

Through narratives such as these, as well as through folktales and fables, we assimilate our world view and value system. For instance, it is unimportant whether George Washington actually chopped down the cherry tree: what is important is that the legend lives and continues to be told. The story reinforces the value we place on honesty and, as such, is told to successive generations of children, who can then see this historical, larger-than-life character as a child who is tempted to lie (such as they might be) but who tells the truth (such as they should). Likewise, it is unimportant whether or not there actually were a Union soldier and a Confederate soldier who faced each other and laid down their guns when they discovered they were both Deaf. What is important is that that legend (which will be examined in the next chapter) is told again and again and reaffirms for the teller and the listener that there is a bond between Deaf people so indivisible that other alliances, no matter how strong, are secondary.

Other forms of folklore serve other functions. Proverbs give us folk wisdom and universal truths passed down in a single sentence or phrase. We learn that we should "live and let live" or, on a more metaphoric level, that a "bird in the hand is worth two in the bush" and that "a rolling stone gathers no moss."

Social customs—from family practices to community observances—provide mechanisms for affirming our membership in such groups and thus establish and reaffirm our identity.

Folk games provide opportunities for learning society's structure and roles. To claim a pile of dirt as your own and to push off anyone who comes onto it is behavior that is socially unacceptable under normal conditions. But if we establish that we're playing "King of the Mountain," it is acceptable. It's just a game, a game that, among other things, enables the child to experience what "success" is in a culture that values competition and individual achievement. Other folk traditions provide the opportunity for particular skills development, such as "Peek-A-Boo," for learning rule structures and object permanence; or "One, two, button my shoe," for learning to count.

In this rapidly changing high-tech world of computers, satellite television and video games, it may be particularly hard for most of us to conceive that American children's folklore still exists, let alone that it has value as an educational tool for the acquisition of kinetic, conceptual, linguistic and social skills. But children's folklore thrives and its forms run the gamut from the purely kinetic to a combination of kinetic and verbal to the purely verbal.

It is obvious that the purely kinetic "tag," "war ball" and "hide 'n seek" promote the development of physical dexterity. The kinetic/verbal play found in jump rope rhymes serves many purposes simultaneously. The classic

> John and Mary sitting in a tree k-i-s-s-i-n-g
> First comes love, then comes marriage
> Then comes Mary with a baby carriage

introduces children to native poetic discourse and gives them the opportunity to practice it. At the same time it offers the opportunity to both "mock and celebrate societal order" (McDowell, 1983: 314-322). It serves the development of language skills and at the same time reaffirms societal values. One of the purely verbal forms, "Riddling," not only provides an opportunity to hone mental dexterity but also puts the riddler in a position of power over the person being riddled. If the person on the receiving end is an adult, the riddling becomes an exciting experiment in reversal for a child.

The lessons to be learned from many of these folk traditions of children can be easily overlooked or misunderstood, because they occur within a play mode, and we often—adults especially—view play as nothing more than that. But researchers in the field have called play such things as "the forerunner of adult competence," "practice for problem-solving and creativity" and "the first business of childhood" (For further discussion see Bruner, Allison & Sylva 1976; Schwartzman, 1978). Play has inherent in it the removal of certain anxieties about achievement and performance. Children in a play situation are not under pressure to succeed and, without that pressure, are thus better able to function—and more receptive to learning. That children's folklore amuses and perhaps even aids the development of physical dexterity is readily apparent. What is less apparent is how children's folklore serves to develop linguistic and social competencies. This we will discover in this chapter's examination of the group narrative.

GROUP NARRATIVE

"Children's narrative produces a verbal icon of a child's experience and, like all narrative, seeks to capture the joy, pathos or mystery of existence" (McDowell, 1983: 317). It provides the primary vehicle from which the development of verbal artistic competence is born. Narratives are the arena from earliest on for the learning of sequencing events to later achieving the sophistication of plot and character development. Among the folk group of Deaf children, one of the most commonly found forms of storytelling is the group narrative. In a group narrative each person has one or more roles. These can be as characters in the story or as props. The story line can be predetermined or can occur spontaneously. The subject matter can range from life experience events—such as a family about to have a Deaf baby—to the borrowed and embellished storyline of a television program or movie. They can be created and performed by as few as two or as many as ten or twelve, two to six participants being more common. Most important, these narratives are developed through the use of the inherent elements of ASL. Though they make use of mime and exaggerated performance, as does adult ASL storytelling, they are, like the narratives of hearing children, sophisticated linguistic expressions.

An excellent example of a ten-person narrative is found in the National Theatre of the Deaf production *My Third Eye*. The play, an original work created by the cast, incorporated traditional forms of sign play, storytelling, creative uses of American Sign Language and personal vignettes of the actors growing up as Deaf children. Together these elements were to give the audience a glimmer of understanding of the Deaf experience and a taste of the richness of the culture of Deaf people. In one scene an example of the traditional form of group narrative is performed, introduced with a remark that tells us much of why this form is so important to Deaf people. "When we were children trying to develop language meaningful to us," the narrator explains, "we invented many stories like this."

Although the following text is from a professional stage performance and not from children in context, I am using this as an illustration of children's group narrative for several reasons. It was created and performed by Deaf adults as a reminiscence of their childhood and it is a clear example of the group narrative structure found in context with Deaf children. From a folklorist's viewpoint, it would be desirable to include the text of any example in this paper in its native language. Since this is impossible, I have chosen the *My Third Eye* example, also, because it is relatively accessible on the videotape recording of the play. Further, several of the Deaf adults whom I interviewed about their reminiscences of group narrative were involved in the creation and performance of this particular text.

THE HELICOPTER RESCUE
English synopsis:

> The scene, involving ten members of the ensemble, starts with the image of the rolling sea and develops into a dramatic rescue by heli-copter of a pilot downed in a storm-tossed sea during wartime. At stage left we see a lighthouse with its beam revolving regularly, sweeping light out over the sea. One actor is the sea, churning with large waves and troughs. On stage right an aircraft carrier emerges, and a plane takes off over the sea. It dramatically commands the sky and swoops left. Suddenly, a battleship appears and its cannon fires at the plane. The plane is hit; the pilot ejects and parachutes into the sea below. The abandoned plane continues in a wide arc and crashes in the distance. The pilot is bobbing on the sea when, from stage left, a rescue helicopter appears. Two actors comprise the helicopter—one the aircraft itself and the other its rescue basket. The basket is lowered, picks up the pilot and reels him into the heli-copter, which then flies off to return to land.

If we use Gilbert Botvin's analysis of plot elements in children's folk narrative (which he adapted from the classic work of Vladimir Propp in Russian folktales) (1977: 145-54) and apply it to this example, we see that the group narrative of Deaf children follows in the same tradition, conforming to the same patterns. For Botvin, the narrative elements of the beginning, middle and end further broke down into subcategories of (beginning) introduction, preparation, complication; (middle) development; (end) resolution and ending. Using our example of "the helicopter rescue," we can see the introduction and the elements preceding the dise-quilibrium as the establishment of the setting: the calm security of the land and the lighthouse beacon; the rolling sea with its potential danger; and the entrance of an aircraft carrier with a plane taking off into the sky. The disequilibrium occurs with the appearance of the battleship and the villainy of the attack on the plane. This is followed by the escape from the threatening situation by the pilot ejecting successfully from the disabled plane, which is about to crash on the horizon. The story is resolved with the rescue of the pilot by helicopter and the safe return to land.

Although the text of this example and the texts of group narratives of Deaf children are not traditional, they are structured similarly to traditional folktales. The same is true for the narratives created by hearing children, as has been noted by Sutton-Smith and his collaborators. In their analysis they found that the narratives generated by hearing children are less well-structured than traditional folktales, legends and myths. They found that children's narratives may also be filled with modern content, such as the themes from television programs, but they "do have the same basic plot structures and the same general concerns with fate, fate overwhelming and fate nullified as do those other genres" (1981: 1-45).

Further, with reference to developing competence in the narrative form, the group narrative serves the same function for the Deaf child that the individual narrative serves for the hearing child. But the Deaf children receive an added benefit because their narrative form takes place within another modality. A hearing child's narrative is inherently linear and more individual because it is spoken. But the Deaf child—operating in a group in a visual modality—learns of cooperation and of simultaneous action. The simultaneity of language production in the Deaf group narrative further provides for a richness of expression both linguistically and stylistically that cannot be duplicated by spoken language. Simultaneous images of weather—such as building thunderheads, lightning, river waters rising and rain washing away river banks—can be signed in unison, producing a very complex linguistic backdrop to, say, a small boy struggling against the elements to warn the town of an impending flood.

An interesting illustration of the linear nature of a spoken narrative was seen in a text collected in studio that was based on an episode of the television program *C.H.I.P.S.* This involved three

Deaf children, two boys and a girl ages 8 and 9. All were from hearing families. One of the boys took on the role of director in addition to his performance duties, and was intent on keeping the others in line with the program they had seen. There was a great amount of detail of character, sets and props especially from the girl, who masterfully captured the episode's femme fatal leaning against a wall while "talking" on a pay telephone call. A straight translation of this defies adequate illumination in writing. The story line was one of a crime was committed, the criminal was apprehended and jailed. A lot of the action focused on the scolding of the criminal by the police for the wrong doing.

Because it was following the visual rendition of the television program, the story was performed one scene at a time. There was little of the cooperative nature and simultaneity of performance typical of other group narratives such as is illustrated in the "Helicopter Rescue."

Not only was this rendition linear, but it proved to be particularly interesting. While it was being performed, their classroom aide, a native signer, and I were having difficulty following the story. For example there would be a scene of someone arrested then sitting in jail with no transition or implied transition. It was as jarring to read in sign as it would have been in English: "Arrest the man, sit in jail." The flatness and lack of fluidity was especially striking in juxtaposition to the extensive visual details and character development. The performance was as disjointed as a string of what filmmakers would call jumpcuts. It wasn't until watching the tape several times that it became obvious that that is exactly what it was. The children's story captured the visual grammar of television but without the complementary audio that together provide the cohesive narrative. Whereas the text may have concerned itself with the same basic plot structures as referred to by Botvin, it was not the same narrative structure as that of the television program. In adhering strictly to the linear nature of the television visual, it lost much of the structure of the group narratives that are of original creation—some of which are based on television characters and storylines, but are not bent on following the television visual frame for frame. An example of structure more typical of the genre is illustrated in the following three-person group poem, which can been seen on the videotape *Creative Uses*

"THE MOUNTAIN POEM"
Three People
(simultaneous images bracketed)

English GLOSS	Person Signing (#) and ASL
A mountain	#1 MOUNTAIN (holding image)
Clouds Snow falling on the mountain	#2 CLOUDS/FALLING SNOW
Sunshine	#3 SUN SHINING ON THE MOUNTAIN
On glistening snow	#2, #3 SPARKLE
Melts into a river and a waterfall	#1, #2, #3 #1, #2, #3
A lake (with a fish) And a duck Quack, quack, quack	#1, #2, #3 WATER SURFACE (LG) (#1 holding image) #2 FISH #3 DUCK (mime quack, quack)
A mountain Sunset	#1 MOUNTAIN (holding image) #3 SUN SETTING BEHIND MOUNTAIN #2 RAYS OF SETTING SUN (behind mountain)
Darken Peace	#1 DARKEN/PEACE

of ASL (Seago, 1980).

Sutton-Smith and his collaborators also noted, using Botvin's techniques to analyze hearing children's individual narrative, that older children demonstrated greater numbers of plot elements: from three elements among five- to six-year-olds, and four among seven- to eight-year-olds, to about six among nine- to ten-year-olds. Although the data collected here did not follow these specific age groups, it did show that the older the Deaf child, the greater the demonstration of plot elements. Among ten- to twelve-year-olds there also appeared to be considerable skill in conveying the visual image and character development of various characters.

Observations of preschool and lower elementary students by Deaf and hearing sign-skilled teachers confirmed that the narrative plot elements demonstrated by these children largely concerned beginnings and endings. This seems further evidence that, while they operate in a different modality, Deaf children functioning within a folk group develop narrative competencies on a par with their hearing contemporaries.

We can see how this holds true for an older, more linguistically sophisticated group of adults in our text example from *My Third Eye*. After the rescue of the pilot, the group narrative moves beyond the concrete to the metaphoric. The sea becomes more tumultuous. The actors' signed narrative tells of a fierce storm with howling wind and relentless rain, crackling lightning and roaring thunder. Then the storm breaks; the sky clears and the violence of the storm transforms into the new hope of a sunrise created by eight of the actors. From one side of the stage comes a bird who flies center and lights calmly on the gently rolling sea. The metaphoric level is more easily understood when the context is known: this piece was created as the long, divisive Vietnam War was coming to an end and hope was high for a brighter, peaceful future.

The development by Deaf children of group narrative does not occur in a vacuum. There are other educative strategies from the folk tradition that assist in narrative development that are brought to the linguistic community of the residential school by Deaf children of Deaf families. Among these are traditional ASL storytelling and sign play skills, customs and pastimes. The following text is from an informant who is widely regarded in the

Deaf community for his storytelling skills. He tells of how his Deaf father would tell stories to the family every evening.

DAD'S STORIES:

THE BUILDING OF THE BAY BRIDGE

Construction of the Bay Bridge lasted from 1933 until 1937 from 1933 making convenient travel between San Francisco and the East Bay possible. My father worked in San Francisco not far from where the bridge building was going on. Every day at noontime he would take his lunch bag and study the construction workers up on the scaffolding erecting the bridge. Before I go on I should explain that at that time they did not use welding. If you recall that hadn't been invented yet. Instead, smooth bolt like rivets were used. They did two beams together, lining up the holes on each, and then stick the bolts through the holes. On each side of the beam stood men whose job it was to drive in the bolts with an air hammer. Well you get the idea. Every day my father would go and watch them. The rivets were kept in a huge caldron set over an open fire that burned all day. When the rivets became red-hot, a man with a pair of tongs would toss one high in the air to the next worker on the scaffolding. That man would then try to scoop the rivet out of the air with a big funnel. And with a pair of clamps quickly shove it into a hole pounding it into place with an air hammer. When all of the rivets were in place and cooled down the beams were locked together. Well, my father enjoyed watching all of this activity. Especially, since the workers had invented their own kind of gestural language, like this...cut at the neck, both hands at waist etc....They used these gestures to communicate because they couldn't hear each other for the racket going on. My father just loved it. It became quite a show. There was no TV in those days. So, my father filled the evenings with his stories of the day's events on the bridge. We could listen to him for hours on end.

There can be little doubt as to the roots of this informant's storytelling skills, skills that when brought to the linguistic community of Deaf children at the residential school must have influenced their skills as well.

That information critical to understanding the story is ex-

plained at the beginning of the narrative is very typical of Deaf
storytelling. Deaf storytellers do not necessarily assume that their
audience has the same base of knowledge that a hearing storytellers might. The hearing individual is continuously bombarded
with information, radio, television, overheard conversation etc.
etc. When we consider that a Deaf person's acquisition of information occurs only through the eyes it cannot be as readily assumed
that there is the same repertoire of knowledge as one can assume
for a hearing audience. With this understanding we can also appreciate the high value that is placed on information by Deaf people. It is the person with information, not necessarily the esoteric
Ph.D. who is the more highly regarded.

Informants overwhelmingly reported that those at school
who "knew things" or "had street smarts" and who could tell stories were highly valued by the group and asked by their peers to
tell stories over and over again. One informant who was not from
a Deaf family, but who had "the knack" and was the best storyteller in his dorm, remembered as an upper elementary student being
asked by his dorm mates to tell them stories. He said that he used
to cut out advertisements for movies that would have a picture on
it and then just make up the story of the movie (his version) without having seen the film. He had quite a devoted audience in the
dorm. "Anyone who could tell stories was very popular with the
others."

Another customary pastime of Deaf people that has been
brought into the residential school by Deaf children that can also
assist in the development of narrative competence is explained as
follows:

T.V./MOVIE STORIES

Before we had captioning on television my family and I would sit and
watch a program or a movie, and when the movie would stop for the
commercials we would all take that time to speculate on the story
and create what was happening and guess at what was going to
happen next. Then at the next break we would see who was right.
We would have great discussions about it. This was not just my family, lots of Deaf families played this game. To be honest, now with
captioning and seeing the dialog I think that a lot of our stories were

better.

Other informants report of doing this at the school where they had televisions in the play room. In my own observations of elementary aged children at the residential school, this was true especially with one group who had a penchant for soap operas. It is also not uncommon to see Deaf people in movie houses signing to each other their ideas of what's happening on screen where there are no sub-titles. This custom, especially when done in Deaf families or other groups with sophisticated language models is excellent skills practice for narrative development.

Another traditional form that assists in sign skill development as well as narrative competency is the sign play One Hand Shape Story. An example follows as illustrated in Figure 13.

THE ARGUMENT

SYNOPSIS:

With a /G/ handshape: Two people bump into each other and argue; but after some consideration they agree to become friends (Seago, 1980: 14).

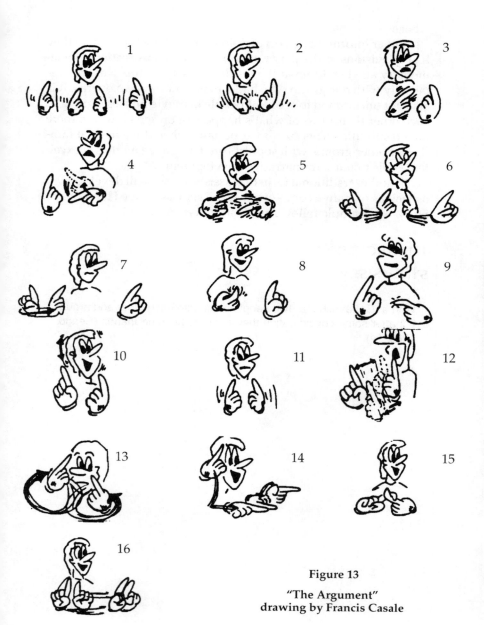

Figure 13

"The Argument"
drawing by Francis Casale

Key to Figure 13

#1 TWO PEOPLE WALKING
#2 BUMP
#3 SCOLDS
#4 INSULTS
#5 ARGUES
#6 LEAVE IN A HUFF
#7 HEY, YOU
#8 COME HERE
#9 WHO ME?
#10 YES, YOU
#11 COME TOGETHER
#12 TALK
#13 RECONSIDER
#14 AGREE
#15 TO BE FRIENDS
#16 WALK AWAY TOGETHER

These traditions from the culture of Deaf people brought into the residential setting by Deaf children from Deaf families surely assist in the development of narrative skills and no doubt aid in the development of sophisticated group narratives. The example of the "Helicopter Rescue" by the NTD cast shows what heights can be reached and what competencies achieved through group narrative. But of what significance is this for Deaf children?

CULTURE AND ENCULTURATION

To date, the focus of Deaf education has been, predominantly, to help Deaf children adapt to the hearing world. This is, of course, a laudable goal since anyone must be able to adapt to society at large in order to succeed and have autonomy over ones life. But too often the specific goal has been to strive for the Deaf child to "become hearing," and that is where this general tendency in Deaf education—whether in a mainstream or residential setting—falls short. When the education system, explicitly or not, holds up spoken English and the mirroring of hearing society as its exclusive goals, it robs Deaf children of their culture. And one's own culture is what enables a person to adapt. Culture is, in itself, a people's adaptive mechanism. It is the sum total that defines a group and enables them to adapt to their environment—and to adjust when thrust into a strange environment.

In our own recent history we have seen what happened when the Bureau of Indian Affairs tried to assimilate Native American children into the larger culture by mainstreaming them in BIA schools. Denied the use of their own language and access to the study of their culture and values, schooled only in English and "white man's ways," these children became misfits—ill-equipped to survive and succeed in either culture, and unwanted by both. The BIA learned that fully functioning Native Americans, grounded in their own culture and proud of their heritage, were in a better position of successfully assimilating into mainstream American culture—if they chose to do so.

Just as sophisticated linguistic competence in a language provides a foundation for achieving competence in a second language, so do cultural and social competencies provide the basis on which one can learn and assimilate other cultures. Culture provides the foundation and the strategies for us to adapt to the world. It establishes our identity. This is no less true for Deaf people as a cultural group. The culture of Deaf people developed—as do all cultures—spontaneously to serve the needs of the people and has been in existence for as long as Deaf people have interacted. It has its own customs and mechanisms suited to meet Deaf people's needs, such as the tradition of name signs (which foster the establishment of identity) or the evolution of educational strategies that enhance skills development. What distinguishes Deaf culture from virtually all others is its pattern of transmission.

For most people of the world, culture is transmitted and learned within the family—passed from parent to child. But, as we have discussed, this is the case for less than ten percent of the Deaf population: the Deaf children from Deaf families. If we equate successful adaptation with leadership in the culture, we can show that the best-adapted among the Deaf come either from this small minority or from the postlingually deaf—those who became deaf after acquiring speech. But the overwhelming majority of the Deaf population fall into neither of these two well-adapted groups: they, instead, are prelingually Deaf children from hearing families, and they are without access to the culture and language of their parents and society at large, and often without access to the folk traditions that have evolved to serve Deaf people.

As folklorist Barre Tolkien points out, it is in the family setting that we develop a sense of us.

> We learn our language, dialect and elemental world view all from hearing and observing other's speech and action. It is in this setting that we note, and participate in certain traditional roles" (1979: 82).

If we extend this understanding to a societal group, our sense of us expands. For the hearing child of hearing parents or the Deaf child of Deaf parents this process develops normally, because in each case both children and parents are functioning within the same language and culture. But for the Deaf child of hearing parents this process is impeded. How does a child without full access to the family's language develop a sense of us? More often than not, the Deaf child in this situation ends up being treated as "the other." Even in the most committed families, in which every effort is made to provide a "total communication" environment, the Deaf children are still somehow different from their siblings, from other children in the neighborhood or school.

It is for children in this group that the school environment is especially crucial, because for them enculturation and language acquisition occurs primarily at the peer level, in the school setting. The educational system, if it recognizes this, can play a pivotal role in helping Deaf children develop to their fullest linguistic and cultural potential.

If we look at some of the primary functions a people's folklore serves—education, reaffirmation of identity, validation of culture and maintenance of conformity to accepted behaviors and norms—we can see the potential folklore has for being useful in meeting the needs of language acquisition and enculturation for the Deaf child. The group narrative under discussion here is but one of the culture's own strategies that aids the development of linguistic competence for the Deaf child simply by providing, among other things, the opportunity to use language in a social context.

We know that through language we become social, but the converse is also true: through being social we learn language. As Garvey points out, "In order to pretend with a companion the child needs techniques for indicating who he is; what he is doing; what objects represent; what objects have been invented; and where he is, at home or at work or on a train" (1977: 86). The highly social nature of dramatic play involving role situation requires the children to actively use language to structure and sustain the play (Garvey, 1977: 86). In fact, in studies of language production in preschool classrooms, "Children have been found to be more verbal in the dramatic play situation than in any other" (Marshall, 1961: 9-15). Interactions that are "real" and meaningful to the child are absolutely essential for the development of language competence and maturity. They must not be ignored for the sake of making time for skills (Scofield, 1978: 719). In focusing on language-delayed children Scofield observes that "to express themselves in imaginative play may be crucial to the development of an affective language repertoire. It may promote the 'stretching' of their ability to deal with things less concrete and immediate than their usual experience" (1978: 723). The social nature of the group narrative not only provides for meaningful and purposeful interaction it also simultaneously provides the matrix for learning social rules and roles.

It is because most children's folklore tends to occur in social activity that it provides the means for the acquisition of social conventions. The rules of the game, the societal definition of roles, the art of negotiating, becoming a cooperating member of a group, and the etiquette necessary to maintain one's membership as a social being, all are part of folklore. Even a session of riddling will not "work" unless ground rules are implicitly agreed upon. Through their folk traditions children are exposed to the culture's basic values and norms. Through the active participation in these activities they develop mastery of them.

The group narrative is but one example of a rich folk tradition of Deaf people and one that serves an effective educative function. Because the deaf education system plays such a powerful and pivotal role in the socialization and enculturation of Deaf children, an understanding of Deaf culture's own strategies for linguistic and cultural development can provide a valuable, if not indispensable educational tool that can give the Deaf children something that is uniquely their own as Deaf people, upon which they can build self-esteem, foster linguistic sophistication, instill values, and develop social skills. All of these are the goals of education. To ignore the culture of Deaf people, one must question if, like the Bureau of Indian Affairs, the educational establishment is cutting off deaf children from their most viable support system and from their greatest educational resource to help them become fully functioning Deaf adults.

---

[5] Hayes, David, director, *My Third Eye*. Composition of the cast of the National Theatre of the Deaf, Waterford, Connecticut, 1971.

[6] No one common term exists among the Deaf Community for this storytelling form. The term "group narrative" has been coined by the author for purposes of description.

CHAPTER V

FOLKLORE AND IDENTITY

The Establishment and Maintenance of the Deaf Identity

Folklore is a particularly useful tool in the study of identity. The unselfconscious expressions of a people through folk materials provide a vivid reflection of their culture and world view, as well as images of group and individual definitions of identity (for a succinct and clear treatise on folklore and identity see Dundes 1985).

Most expositions on the nature of identity refer to the concepts of self-sameness, a continuity with one's past, and the idea that personal and social identities are defined also by identifying who we are not: "the other" (Erikson 1968; Mead, 1934; Dundes, 1985). This chapter will examine Deaf identity through these concepts as reflected in folk materials. It will also examine the importance for an oppressed minority of the establishment and maintenance of identity, and it will illuminate the process of reaffirmation of the Deaf cultural identity.

On the idea of identity Erikson says, "The conscious feeling of having a personal identity is based on two simultaneous observations: the perception of self-sameness and continuity of one's existence in time and space and the perception of the fact that others recognize one's sameness and continuity" (1968:50).

This perception of one's identity as reflected by others revolves largely around a process of mirroring. Cooley describes this as "the looking glass self" (1964). (See also Greenacre, 1958: 613; De Levita 1965: 150; Luckmann 1979: 66, 72.) The individual's image of self develops and is internalized largely from the image the individual sees that others have of him.

Individual and social or group identities, the "who we are," both develop also through a determining of "who we are not," the establishment of "the other" (Mead, 1934). "There can be no self without other, no identity of Group A without a Group B" (Dundes, 1985: 238).

An illustration of Deaf self-sameness and continuity with a past and the establishment of the other, in this case the hearing world, can be seen in the following legends and personal narrative related to Deaf people, the Civil War and Abraham Lincoln.

Brundvand notes that cycles of legends cluster around dramatic events in a nation's history. "In the United States, legend cycles have developed around the Revolutionary War, the Civil War, the Indian Wars and the settlement of the frontier" (1968: 99). So it is not surprising that we would find Deaf American legends relating to the Civil War. What better way to validate one's continuity and link with the past than to be able to place one's people in a widely recognized part of the nation's heritage.

There are many stories told of Deaf participation in the war, but, the historical record of actual participation is scant. Jack Gannon in Deaf Heritage states that "three or four Deaf or hard-of-hearing men served in the war as soldiers. One was William Simpson, the hard-of-hearing brother of Delos and James Simpson, who were Deaf. William decided to join the Northern cause during the outbreak of war. He realized that he and his hearing impairment were too well known in his hometown so he went to New York to enlist. He served throughout the war, then returned home to become a farmer." Gannon further notes, "One account tells of a Deaf Confederate prisoner of war whose guard was also Deaf. The two carried on a lively conversation in sign language" (1980: 10). The record also shows that one Hartwell M. Chamberlayne, who was born deaf, had served in the infantry, cavalry and artillery of the Confederacy. After the war he became a teacher at the Virginia School for the Deaf. And from Gannon again, we find "a man named William M. Berkeley, who 'managed to get mixed up in the Civil War in spite of his deafness.' ...He served in the Confederate Army with the Augusta Rifle Company, which was attached to the 25th Virginia Regiment" (1980: 10).

The connection with history, the strength of sign language as a major identifying characteristic of Deaf people and the existence of the other in the form of the hearing world can be seen in the following Civil War legend.

CIVIL WAR SOLDIERS

During the Civil War, there was a time when they did not have enough soldiers and they were recruiting everyone. They didn't care if you were deaf or not; it didn't matter. So it happened that there was this Northern Deaf soldier and a Southern Deaf soldier. The Northern Deaf soldier was very lonely. He couldn't sit and chat or interact with the other men in his company. Without any other Deaf people there, he was alone, isolated. The Southern Deaf soldier was experiencing the same thing, sitting around camp, not doing anything and not being a part of the group. One day the battle lines between the North and South got closer and closer. The Northern Deaf soldier decided to go for a walk in the woods. To his astonishment he came upon the Southern Deaf soldier. He drew his gun, as did the Southern Deaf soldier. They stood there uncomfortably holding their guns on each other and began to gesture nervously. Then one soldier asked in sign, "Are you Deaf?" The other soldier responded, "Yes! Yes!" The first soldier said, "Same as me. We're both Deaf!" "Same as me," signed the second soldier. Delighted to have found each other, they quickly put their guns away and began to chat and chat and chat.

Soon some of the men in the Northern Deaf soldier's company noticed that he was missing from camp and began to search for him. The same thing occurred in the Southern camp and a group of Confederate soldiers began searching for the Southern Deaf soldier. Both groups happened on the two Deaf soldiers at the same time. Each group suspected espionage but did not know who the traitor was. Which one was telling the secrets? Which one was getting the information? Both groups drew their weapons on the Deaf men. The Deaf soldiers quickly communicated, "No, no, we're Deaf, that's all, just talking with each other." They pleaded with their respective search parties to keep it a secret—not to tell their superiors, as they were just happy to see another Deaf person and be able to share in communication and some food and drink. They begged that their actions not be misunderstood and insisted that they were not guilty of treason, a crime for which they would certainly be hung. They so convinced the hearing soldiers that both groups stayed with the Deaf men and socialized, ate and drank together into the night. Afterward, each group went back to its respective camp.

It seems that somehow the superiors at the Northern camp found out about their men socializing with Southern soldiers. At this point the story is a bit unclear. It seems, however, that Abraham Lincoln read a report about the Deaf soldiers meeting, because it is said that he really admired the two Deaf men. He saw them as very wise men who were able to put the war aside and be attentive to something more important— human communication and brotherhood. He felt that if they were wise enough to see this, that they should not be reprimanded.

Sometime later, President Lincoln was signing a number of bills. Among them was the one asking for the establishment of Gallaudet University. He might normally have thought that this was an unimportant and inconsequential bill, but he remembered the incident from the battlefield and how he so admired those Deaf men and their display of brotherhood. So, he immediately signed the bill, and that is how Gallaudet University was established.

This legend is a strong illustration of Deaf identity transcending all others. Within popular literature and legend, the Civil War is a classic context for the conflict of opposites: black and white, North and South, Union and Confederate. These conflicts were strong enough to split families along philosophical lines. And yet, even more powerful than the group identities established by being on one side or the other of this historic conflict is the identity that Deaf people share. For this legend to be set in the Civil War makes this illustration of transcendence particularly pointed.

This particular text was collected during an interview session in which the informant was discussing the kinds of things she would like to present in a ASL storytelling performance for a Deaf audience. Her purpose for such a performance was two-fold. One was certainly to amuse and be entertaining and the other was to pass on the information about Deaf culture to other Deaf people. She saw a great need for more of this to occur. "Many Deaf people don't realize that they have such a history." She herself had seen this story told by a Deaf man at a National Association of the Deaf convention. "We were all just sitting there astonished at it and we so enjoyed it. It was a wonderful story."

The story certainly reaffirms the self-samenesss aspect of Deaf identity. When the soldiers discover that they are both Deaf, they signed "same as me" (SAME-SAME). When the two soldiers discovered they were both Deaf, "they quickly put their guns away." Holding a gun on an enemy soldier might be acceptable behavior in the context of war, however, for Deaf people to hold guns on each other is not acceptable behavior. Like most other minority groups, Deaf folks tend to support fellow members and are less likely to exhibit behaviors to the contrary. After the guns were put away they began to "chat and chat and chat." This is precisely what Deaf people would tend to do in this situation. Because the language is one that requires face to face contact for communication to occur, when Deaf people meet there is a great tendency to put all other business aside and talk. Again, the reverence for human communication is paramount.

Positive reaffirmation of identity is seen in the story when it is the Deaf men who bring the groups of Union and Confederate soldiers together. The story illustrates typical Deaf experience: when a Deaf person is alone in a group of hearing people, he is isolated, not interacting or participating at a meaningful level. But here in this story, when the Deaf men come together, they are able to accomplish great things on a very meaningful level. Being able to bring the North and South together—a feat that no one else was able to do—is an enormously powerful image of the worth of Deaf people. Further, it is not just Deaf people who might retell this story reaffirming this idea, but Abraham Lincoln as well. What greater confirmation of the truth of these facts could a storyteller want.

Abraham Lincoln holds a special place in the hearts of Deaf people, perhaps because he signed the bill in 1864 that led to the creation of Gallaudet University. Lincoln also had an earlier involvement in the establishment of the Illinois School for the Deaf when he was a legislator in that state in 1846.

Furthermore, there is a special reverence for the Lincoln Memorial among some Deaf people, and it is the focus of the following popular Deaf urban legend.

DANIEL FRENCH AND THE LINCOLN MEMORIAL

The sculptor who did the likeness of Abraham Lincoln at the Lincoln Memorial was Daniel Chester French. French also sculpted the Thomas Hopkins Gallaudet and Alice Cogswell Memorial statue for Gallaudet University. If you look at the hands of Abraham Lincoln's statue they are posed in the handshapes of "A" and "L" of the manual alphabet. Lincoln is sitting there signing his initials (see Figure 14).

The Gallaudet/Cogswell memorial statue is a famous work within the Deaf community. It is often seen in pictures or other illustrations representing Gallaudet University. It is a very familiar image. Figure 15 is an engraving of the statue that appeared in the September 1889 issue of The Silent Worker. The statue clearly shows Gallaudet teaching his first pupil, Cogswell, the letter "A." There is no record of French ever acknowledging that he purposely sculpted Lincoln's hands to depict the president's initials. However, the existence of this previous work of Gallaudet and Cogswell lends believability to the legend of French's Lincoln Memorial work, and assists in the believability of the story.

Figure 14
The Sitting Lincoln

Figure 15
Gallaudet and Cogswell Memorial Statue

French also sculpted a bust of President James A. Garfield, which is displayed at Gallaudet University. It stands in Chapel Hall, where Garfield made his last public address. Garfield also was a champion of Deaf people. When he was in Congress he was a strong ally of Gallaudet University and his death was a tragic loss keenly felt by Deaf people.

But although he was a supporter of Deaf people and martyred by assassination, as was Lincoln, there doesn't seem to be the same sort of larger-than-life images of him within Deaf folklore that there are of Lincoln.

Lincoln seems to occupy a cherished place in the hearts of Deaf people for another reason. On a visit to Washington, D. C., a Deaf friend took me to the Lincoln Memorial. We looked at the hands. They did appear to be roughly in the handshapes of "A" and "L," and it was possible with a little stretch to imagine that Lincoln was signing his initials. However, my friend soon directed my attention to the inscription of the Gettysburg Address on the wall across from 'The Sitting Lincoln' to the left (see Figure 16).

FOUR SCORE AND SEVEN YEARS
AGO OUR FATHERS BROUGHT FORTH
ONTHIS CONTINENT A NEW NATION
CONCEIVED IN LIBERTY AND DEDICA-
TED TO THE PROPOSITION THAT ALL
MEN ARE CREATED EQUAL •
NOW WE ARE ENGAGED IN A GREAT
CIVIL WAR TESTING WHETHER THAT
NATION OR ANY NATION SO CON-
CEIVED AND SO DEDICATED CAN LONG
ENDURE • WE ARE MET ON A GREAT
BATTLEFIELD OF THAT WAR• WE HAVE
COME TO DEDICATE A PORTION OF
THAT FIELD AS A FINAL RESTING
PLACE FOR THOSE WHO HERE GAVE
THEIR LIVES THAT THAT NATION
MIGHT LIVE • IT IS ALTHOGETHER FIT-
TING AND PROPER THAT WE SHOULD
DO THIS • BUT IN A LARGER SENSE
WE CAN NOT DEDICATE~WE CAN NOT
CONSECRATE~WE CAN NOT HALLOW~
THIS GROUND • THE BRAVE MEN LIV-
ING AND DEAD WHO STRUGGLED HERE
HAVE CONSECRATED IT FAR ABOVE
OUR POOR POWER TO ADD OR DETRACT
THE WORLD WILL LITTLE NOT NOR
LONG REMEMBER WHAT WE SAY HERE
BUT IT CAN NEVER FORGET WHAT THEY
DID HERE • IT IS FOR US THE LIVING
RATHER TO BE DEDICATED HERE TO
THE UNFINISHED WORK WHICH THEY
WHO FOUGHT HERE HAVE THUS FAR
SO NOBLY ADVANCED•IT IS RATHER FOR
US TO BE HERE DEDICATED TO THE
GREAT TASK REMAINING BEFORE US-
THAT FROM THESE HONORED DEAD
WE TAKE INCREASED DEVOTION TO
THAT CAUSE FOR WHICH THEY GAVE THE
LAST FULL MEASURE OF DEVOTION ~
THAT WE HERE HIGHLY RESOLVE THAT
THESE DEAD SHALL NOT HAVE DIED IN
VAIN~THAT THIS NATION UNDER GOD
SHALL HAVE A NEW BIRTH OF FREEDOM~
AND THAT GOVERNMENT OF THE PEOPLE
BY THE PEOPLE FOR THE PEOPLE SHALL
NOT PERISH FROM THE EARTH•

Figure 16
THE GETTYSBURG ADDRESS
Southeast wall of the Lincoln Memorial
My friend explained that she found these words very inspira-

tional. Our attention fixed on the inscription. The legend of the handshape initials faded in importance. When I told this to other Deaf friends and colleagues who knew the memorial, they too talked more of the inscription than of the statue. The handshaped initials made for an interesting and, for some, a mildly amusing story, but the importance of the memorial to them as Deaf people was found more in the inscription.

Lincoln obviously understood and cared about the human needs of oppressed people. His ideals were humane; he was the emancipator of slaves. He himself overcame humble beginnings to achieve the highest office in the land. He was a larger-than-life figure whose reputation for speaking the truth was legend. And here at the memorial are expressed the ideals of equality, self-governance and freedom for all humankind, which most certainly includes Deaf people. Further, these sentiments are engraved in marble in the center of Washington for all to see. It is a powerful validation for all oppressed people, and particularly meaningful to an oppressed group that was personally touched by Lincoln. Washington, D.C., has one of the nation's largest concentrations of Deaf people, due to the presence of Gallaudet University and to the many opportunities for employment in federal jobs such as the Government Printing Office and the Postal service. With its many public monuments and displays, Washington also serves as a focal point for our country's heritage. People visiting there can connect with their identity as Americans and see a continuity with their past. Deaf people have a strong connection to the city and its heritage via Gallaudet University. The legends about Lincoln and the Lincoln Memorial serve as a further point of meaningful connection with all that is public Washington for Deaf Americans. The memorial's presence is a continual reaffirmation of the validity of Deaf people and their inclusion in American society.

Another Civil War story, told by a Deaf woman about her grandfather and written by her in a paper titled "It Happened During the Civil War," this was also recounted by Gannon (1980: 9) under the title "Sign Language Saves a Life." This story also serves nicely as a connection with history and illustrates contrasts between culturally determined behaviors of Deaf and hearing people. That the story is told from a Deaf point of view is evident.

SIGN LANGUAGE SAVES A LIFE

Eighteen-year-old Joshua Davis was squirrel hunting one day on his parents' southern plantation near Atlanta, Georgia, during the Civil War. Suddenly he found himself surrounded by Union soldiers. Davis was deaf but he could tell that they were shouting at him. The soldiers were members of General Sherman's army, which was marching to the sea destroying everything in its path.

Davis pointed to his ears and gestured that he was deaf, but the soldiers did not believe him. They suspected that he was a spy and was trying to fool them by pretending to be deaf. They shoved and pushed the youth to a nearby house. A couple standing in front of the house informed them that the youth was their son and that he was, indeed, deaf. The captors did not believe them either and they were looking for a rope to hang young Davis as a spy when a mounted officer rode up. The officer was informed that they had caught a spy who was "playing deaf." The officer rode over to the youth and fingerspelled to him: "Are you deaf?" The youth responded in signs, "Yes." "Where were you educated?" the officer asked next, to which the young man told him, the school for the deaf in Cave Spring. With that information the officer ordered the youth released and the family's house spared.

Greatly relieved at the unexpected turn of events the family invited the officer to dine with them. During the meal the officer and Joshua Davis conversed in sign language. The family learned that the officer had a deaf brother in Illinois who had taught him to talk with his hands.

Joshua Davis later moved to Texas, became a farmer and raised a family of seven. Five of his children were deaf and one was hard of hearing. He lived to the age of 84, never forgetting how close he came to being hanged when he was only 18.

The officer knew the two major identifying characteristics of Deaf people—the use of sign language and attendance at a residential school. No two more telling questions could have been asked in order to identify Joshua Davis as being Deaf. The fact that the officer knew how to sign and just what to ask also identified him as someone who had some connection with Deaf people, not just a "hearing other." Especially at this point in history, it would be most unlikely to find hearing people who knew sign language without some immediate connection to its community. Since the officer's experience with deafness was based in the signing, culturally Deaf community, it was indeed fortunate that Joshua was of the same

> identity and not merely audiologically deaf. Had that been the case, the story might have had another outcome. Joshua would have had to demonstrate the major identifying characteristic of an inability to hear, which he was already having difficulty doing. This part of the story is a nice reaffirmation of the value of signing.

That this story is told from a Deaf perspective is obvious in several ways. There is no explanation or rationalization as to why a Union officer would accept the invitation of a Confederate family to dine in their home. From a Deaf point of view there would be no need to explain. The hearing parents of Joshua share the same familial tie with the Deaf community as does the officer. The parents have a signing Deaf son; the officer, a signing Deaf brother. The fact that the officer was Union was incidental to the fact that he and Joshua Davis were connected by language. The use of sign language, more than the degree of impaired hearing, is the link. As seen in the earlier legend, the connection to the culturally Deaf community transcends the ties to North or South. In this respect both the officer and the parents are more closely following Deaf cultural norms, which place a high value on communication whenever the opportunity presents itself and on the facilitating of that communication. It would be most appropriate to stay and chat, at the very least to share the biographical information that would explain why the officer, a hearing person, knew intimate details of Deaf life. To stay for dinner would be most natural in a Deaf context.

Other evidence of a Deaf point of view in this story is the mention of how the Union officer learned sign language. "The family learned that the officer had a Deaf brother in Illinois who had taught him to talk with his hands." A hearing accounting would more likely refer to the officer as having "learned" sign because he had a deaf brother—the hearing person projected as active, the deaf person as passive. In fact, as Deaf people know well, it is usually the opposite. Hearing people learn sign language through a lot of giving effort on the part of Deaf individuals, who are rarely credited for their work. While the credit for the teaching by Deaf individuals is often overlooked, the general public praises the hearing learner, who is now in the position of "helping the poor Deaf person." This irony is certainly not missed by the Deaf world. A hearing rendering of this story might also add in the concluding paragraph that Joshua Davis later moved to Texas, became a farmer and raised a family of seven "in spite of his handicap." The further accounting of how many of the children were deaf and how many were hard of hearing is essential Deaf biographical information and its inclusion is typically Deaf.

As in the previous legend, hearing people represent the other. There are Northern soldiers and Southern soldiers and Deaf soldiers. Although the officer was hearing in this story, there was a qualitative difference between him and the other hearing soldiers. He was hearing, but could sign and had some connection with the Deaf community. The parents were also hearing, but in this story were not portrayed as totally outside of the Deaf world, as the soldiers were. So there are qualitative differences in the identification of the hearing other.

Baker and Cokely use the term Deaf community to refer to the Deaf cultural world as well as to an extended unit of people involved in deafness. They suggest that there are four avenues of membership in this extended Deaf community—audiological, linguistic, social and political. The audiological avenue refers to the hearing impairment; the linguistic to the ability to sign; social to interaction with Deaf people; and the political to being involved in the political realm on behalf of deaf people (1980: 56). As noted in their diagram, Figure 17, the boundaries of each of these spheres is marked by attitude. This diagram is useful in describing the relationship of the hearing officer to the Deaf world. He would be seen here as a member of the larger more extended Deaf community by virtue of linguistic and social avenues of membership. He could sign and had socialized and interacted with Deaf people. So, although hearing, he was also identified as being a member of the larger Deaf community.

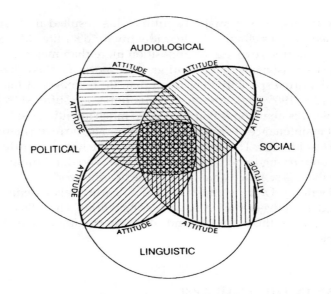

Figure 17
Avenues of Membership
in the Extended Deaf Community

It is important to one's sense of identity—personal or group—to define what one is. But equally important to identity is to define what one is not. Thus far, we have seen illustrations of this with "Deaf" being "not hearing." Broadly, the in-group is Deaf/not hearing; the out-group is hearing/not Deaf.

These definitions of in-group and out-group are critical for the maintenance of the minority identity. For Spicer it is this oppositional process that creates what he refers to as "persistent identity systems" (1971: 797). This is especially true for a minority group that is not seen as a collective people by the majority, but whose members, rather, are defined by the hearing majority as being isolated individuals with a hearing problem. The majority world controls the institutions that in turn control the education, socialization and enculturation of the majority of Deaf people. Dundes states that "the persecution of minority cultures (for example,

Jews, blacks, etc.) by majority cultures has resulted in these oppressed peoples clinging to their identity for dear life...Moreover,
since minorities experience opposition more than majorities, it is
perfectly reasonable that minorities have more of a stake in defining identity (especially their own) than do members of majority
cultures" (1985: 239). With the added oppression suffered by Deaf
people, it is no wonder that there is so much attention paid to the
strict maintenance of group boundaries and to the reaffirmation of
the Deaf identity. This befuddles much of the hearing world who
"are only trying to help Deaf people" and who don't understand
why there is so much animosity to the hearing world.

   Defining Deaf by illustrating the hearing other defines the
boundary between the Deaf and hearing worlds. The following fable delineates this boundary and addresses the oppression of Deaf
people.

DEAF IN THE YEAR 2000

Months have passed since the first Deaf astronaut lost contact with
Earth. He lands on a planet and finds that the people on it are
Deaf....They explain to him that they don't need telephones, they
use video phones signing to each other on TV. Their movies are
signed and they have Deaf newscasters.
The astronaut says, "It sure is different on Earth. There the Hearing
are the majority and the Deaf, the minority. How do hearing people
get along here?"
"Oh those poor hearing people, they suffer so much," says the
guide. "They're fighting for their civil rights. They have a National
Association of the Hearing; a telephone interpreting relay service
and a Hearing Counseling Advocacy and Referral Agency, which
helps hearing people who are frustrated looking for a job. It's rough
for 'em. We Deaf teach 'em, give them legal advice, counsel them
and help them find a job." "Oh, that's really interesting..."
Everywhere they go, everyone is signing. The guide nudges the
astronaut. "Wanna see something? Take a look at this." The astronaut looks up at a marquee flashing "The Hearing Club." "This is
really funny. Come on in. I've gotta show you this. It's hysterical!"
They go into the club. It's really dark inside and they can feel the
floor vibrate. The astronaut asked, "What's this? This is really

strange." "Oh, this is what they call music." Then they look around the room and see all the people's moving mouths. "That's how they communicate," says the guide. He continues, "Oh, look," and they look over to the stage where there is a woman, who is a real "bombshell" with her mouth wide open and her eyes fluttering and doing this: aaaahhhhhhyyyyyaaaaaa (a portrait of a dramatic songstress follows. The characterization includes a detailed graphic portrayal of her open mouth including an exaggerated glottis vibrating intensely). After an extensive tour of the Planet of the Deaf, the Deaf astronaut takes off for home. Meanwhile, back on Earth. NASA is going crazy. They've just spotted a U.F.O. Could it be the lost shuttle with our Deaf astronaut? Will he be alive? Will his body be intact? Will he be sane? These and more questions would have to go unanswered for the moment...

The shuttle lands safely. All Earth anxiously awaits...the hatch opens and out pops the long-lost astronaut.

"Look, he's alive! After all these months, how is it possible?" The president of the National Association of the Deaf (NAD) greets him. He steps forward and begins recounting his adventures on the Planet of the Deaf and delivers to all Deaf Americans the invitation from the Planet of the Deaf to join them in their world. He says, "I urge you to consider this invitation because things here on Earth will get worse; services will be cut, and there will be more oppression. Again, I urge you to leave." And the Deaf people looked at him with new hope.

This text was collected in the San Francisco Bay Area at a time when federal and state fiscal cutbacks were seriously affecting health and human service programs, education and the arts—all of which are major sources of support for Deaf programs.

The transposition of Deaf and hearing worlds in the fable reveal much of how Deaf people view a hearing perception of them. References such as "those poor hearing people" who "suffer so much" and how "we Deaf teach 'em, give them legal advice, counsel them and help them find a job" all speak to the patronization that Deaf people feel from the hearing world. It is not a resentment toward the services themselves. We can see in the concluding statement of the astronaut that the cuts in such services is equated with more oppression of Deaf folks. But the resentment is related to the attitude of the hearing service provider.

Another illustration of the superior attitude of the hearing other is seen in the following text of an imitation of a teacher.

THE COOKING TEACHER

At the School for the Deaf in Kansas some of the other students and I made a pastime of imitating our teachers. I chose my favorite, the cooking teacher, who was hearing. Watch this. (The physical demeanor transforms to a pompous, raised carriage, stiff posture, snooty expression—that of someone who definitely regards her station as much higher than that of her students. The performance uses exaggerated mouth movements of a hearing teacher who is using some sign and fingerspelling as she speaks. The performer does not use her voice).

Ahhem, (clearing throat) today, we will talk about the etiquette of serving. Now we will...I will explain how to hold, yes, serve, the plate. Voila, the plate. Pleeeese do not put your thumbs like this ..(over the lip of the plate holding it more like a frisbee). This is veeerrry bad. Put your plate....you lay it, you lay it on your fingers like this...et voila. It's very easy. Easy, E-A-S-Y. Ahemmmm.

Imitations are a traditional pastime of children at the residential school and can also be seen at Deaf adult gatherings where skits or other entertainment are being performed. In my early collecting of these, they seemed always to be a biting characterization of hearing teachers or other staff. On interview with informants I asked if the mocking of hearing outsiders was not the main reason for the characterizations. The imitations seemed to this hearing observer to be an outlet for hostile feelings toward an oppressor. However, interviews with informants did not bear out this simplistic explanation. Deaf people were also fair game for the imitators, and a few imitations were done in a very loving way, pointing out positive qualities as well. Informants generally agreed that it was the pompousness or other character flaws that were being mocked. Interestingly, further collecting and interview bore out the observation that imitations of people who were "awfully hearing" and terribly oppressive were just not done. They were relegated to the ultimate in deprecation—they simply did not exist.

The informant's analysis of The Cooking Teacher follows:
Imitating the teachers and counselors began in the classroom,

where we were dying of boredom. We had to watch them all day anyway. We took that opportunity to really study them—their every move and gesture. Then I would go home and I would practice until I had them down perfectly. Later in class, or rather the playroom, I would get the attention of all of the kids by flicking the lights on and off. I'd ask, "Who am I imitating?" and then go into my act. They'd all try to guess who it was. I liked that. It was so much better than just sitting through a boring class. I loved imitating the teachers. A few of us kids were really good at it.

That the Deaf/hearing boundary is more subtle than a distinction of auditory ability is illustrated in the relationship of hearing children of Deaf parents to the Deaf community. A look at this relationship might further define the Deaf/hearing boundary. The following joke involves a Deaf person, a hearing person and a child of Deaf parents.

THE SPEEDING DEAF DRIVER

Here's a story about a hearing hitchhiker and a Deaf driver. This Deaf guy is driving along and picks up a hitchhiker on the highway. Then, he continues cruising at his usual 80 miles per hour. Well, before you know it they get pulled over. The hitchhiker is thinking "Oh, no, we're in for it now." The cop comes up to the car and the driver signs "I'm Deaf." And the cop, chagrinned, says, "O.k., but, take it easy....not so fast, o.k.?" and sends the driver on his way. As soon as the cop is out of sight, the guy floors it again, and a second time they get pulled over. The hitchhiker thinks, "Boy, what's going on here?" When the second cop approaches, the driver again gestures, indicating, "I'm Deaf." The cop only reprimands him and tells him to slow down etc. etc. and sends him on his way. The hitchhiker thinks, "Boy, the Deaf sure have got it made." After a while the driver get tired and asks the hitchhiker to take over. "Oh, boy, gladly." So soon he's traveling the speed of light, when the sirens blare. He is ready with his story. He looks at the cop and signs, "I'm Deaf." And in fluent sign language the cop replies, "So were my parents," and writes out the ticket.

To look at this joke in terms of defining in-group and out-group membership, we see that the hearing child of Deaf parents is included in the in-group. In fact, he is the one who catches and humiliates the hearing person by virtue of his signing skills. Many hearing children have native competence in ASL equal to their Deaf parents, and for a substantial number ASL is their first language. One might assume that accompanying this native competency in the language would be a Deaf cultural competency as well, and that this would ensure membership in the Deaf world. However, the situation is not that clear. Hearing children of Deaf parents have a bilingual/bicultural identity that is not formally recognized or generally understood by either Deaf or hearing worlds.

Indicative of their status is the fact these hearing offspring interacted a great deal with the Deaf community as children, but less so as they approached courting age. Many children of Deaf parents recall pleasant memories of socializing with other Deaf people as children. They would often accompany their parents to the Deaf club and other activities central to the community. However, this inclusion in Deaf events and activities seems to taper off at adolescence. This pattern is consistent with other cultural groups, who may permit their children to interact with "outsiders" until the time when courting or marriage is at hand. At a recent conference of Children of Deaf Adults (CODA) there was a general consensus of the two hundred plus participants that their Deaf parents discouraged them from interacting with Deaf people of the opposite sex when they reached adolescence. From this information alone we can see that hearing children of Deaf parents may be to some degree culturally Deaf, but they are also hearing and considered an outsider to the Deaf experience. Study of this phenomenon could shed valuable light on the understanding of a bicultural cultural identity. It could also provide valuable help in defining the Deaf identity (for further discussion see Rutherford and Jacobs, 1987).

The border of Deaf and hearing worlds is not the only boundary that shapes Deaf identity. Another area where we see what Deaf is not—and therefore can see what it is—is in the defining of the "oral other." This is a person who is deaf, but who adheres more to the oral philosophy. The oral other, although audiologically deaf, is more aligned with the hearing world. An illustration of this is seen in the skit "The Operating Room."

Long a popular genre in the folk tradition of Deaf people, skits are often put together and performed at Deaf gatherings by young and old alike. The gathering may be a social event in the home, an afternoon play activity in the residential school game room or a Saturday night at the Deaf club.

"The Operating Room" is a skit in traditional form that humorously portrays the surgical removal from an oral deaf person of that which does not belong in a Deaf person and the replacement of that which does. It was performed in 1980 as part of the play Tales From A Clubroom at the Centennial Celebration of the National Association of the Deaf in Cincinnati. Written by two Deaf men, Bernard Bragg and Eugene Bergman, it was performed to a Deaf and hearing audience in sign only. There was no attempt to translate or voice the performance for nonsigners. It was a play by Deaf people, about Deaf people, for Deaf people. It was very well received by the Deaf audience. Conversations and interview with audience members afterward revealed general agreement that the play captured what "Deaf" is. It was so accurate a picture of a slice of the Deaf world that a detailed examination is warranted here.

The context: the setting is a typical Deaf club. The Deaf club has a long history within the folk tradition of Deaf America and is described by the authors thusly:

> In any city, the club of the deaf is the heart of the deaf community. It is the principal meeting place and forum of the deaf. It is in most cases, the only place where they can socialize. It is their ballroom, their bar, their motion picture house, their theatre, their coffeehouse, their community center—all rolled into one. It is a piece of their own land in exile—an oasis in the world of sound.

Deaf people with whom I discussed the play generally agreed that Bragg and Bergman's list of characters comprised a wonderfully detailed cross-section of Deaf people and portrayed exactly the diverse types who would have been at the Deaf club. They are offered here to set the context of audience and players for "The Operating Room" skit. (Note also the character of Evelyn Jackson, the only hearing person in the play, is a hearing child of Deaf parents. Her marital status is also clearly described as spinster.)

CHARACTERS

Jim Yakubski - Club treasurer, peacemaker, legal counselor.

Ida Yakubski - His wife, a motherly lady who is responsible for coffee and sandwiches.

Abe Greene - Club president; uses salty language and has a domineering manner; always chomping on a cigar.

Kathy Greene - His wife, an excitable, lively woman; a drama fan, always on the go; thinks of skits as the most sophisticated form of drama.

Mark Lindsey - Young graduate of Gallaudet University; signs "Englishy," that is with English syntax.

Shirley Klaymans - Thrice-divorced blonde; shapely, fun-lover, laughs easily.

Mary Brannon - Club deadbeat; a mannish young woman with a savage, furtive manner.

Will Grady - Operator of the club's movie projector; wears a suit and bow tie, unlike most others; laughs readily, the club's jokester.

Tim Shalleck - Muscular bartender with limited education; he uses only the simplest and most picturesque signs.

Janice Wiseman - Garrulous, alcoholic widow.

Willie Futrell - TTY repairman; an earnest man.

Jean Futrell - His wife; a spitfire of a woman who loves to gossip.

Charles Carswell - ABC (manual alphabet) card peddler; flashy dresser, self-assured.

Winona Shoemaker - A young girl; a recent graduate of a school for the deaf.

Gary McAllister - Light on his feet, a basketball player.

Jay Macher - Old-time basketball coach.

Thomas Spivey - Club pariah; with a fixed grin on his face, he somehow manages to be near the focus of most conversations without ever saying anything himself.

Evelyn Jackson - Hearing spinster; the daughter of deaf parents; feels comfortable with the deaf and likes to consort with them.

Alan Ballin - Native young man with tunnel vision (Usher's Syndrome).

Spencer Collins - Young ex-oralist, signs awkwardly

The skit:

THE OPERATING ROOM
MRS. GREENE
(To Everyone.) We saved the best for last. Our next skit is called

"The Operating Room." I've got a bottle of smelling salts in my purse for any man, woman, or child who faints. People sensitive to the sight and smell of blood are advised to close their eyes during this skit.
(MRS. GREENE and MRS. WISEMAN carry on two sawhorses and set them up. GRADY and MACHER enter wearing surgical outfits and carrying KLAYMANS on a board covered up with a white sheet; only her head is visible. The board is laid on the two sawhorses. MRS. WISEMAN is also in a surgical outfit and assisting as a nurse.)

FIRST DOCTOR (To NURSE.) Pass me the scalpel.

NURSE (To FIRST DOCTOR.) I don't know what it is.
SECOND DOCTOR (To FIRST DOCTOR.) You spelled the word wrong. S-C-A-L-P-E-L.

FIRST DOCTOR (To SECOND DOCTOR.) Oh! (To NURSE.) Scalpel!

NURSE (Looking around for it. To FIRST DOCTOR.) I still don't know what it looks like.

(FIRST DOCTOR describes it in gestures.)

NURSE Oh, that! OK! (Picks up imaginary knife and hands to FIRST DOCTOR.) (The actors are joking about the contrast between gesture, which the doctor immediately understands and fingerspelling, which relies on English.)

(FIRST DOCTOR proceeds to cut the patient, who is kicking and screaming, and moving her head.)

SECOND DOCTOR (To FIRST DOCTOR.) Oh, God! We forgot to put her to sleep. (He mimes giving the PATIENT a mask to cover face and turning on the ether. PATIENT grows quiet.)

(FIRST DOCTOR makes a ripping, slicing motion, then plunges his arm into PATIENT'S stomach, searches and extricates a hearing aid, which he lifts high for all to see, and whose function he mimes.)

FIRST DOCTOR What's that? A hearing aid?

NURSE The patient is deaf.

FIRST DOCTOR And dumb! She swallowed it, thinking it would help her hear. (Laughs. Puts hearing aid into NURSES'S hands.)

(FIRST DOCTOR then draws out in succession a microphone, a portable radio, and a loudspeaker, all of which he displays to the AUDIENCE. He then hands one after another to the NURSE.)

SECOND DOCTOR Look! (He plunges his hand into the PATIENT'S body and draws out a tongue.) She's an oralist. She used that tongue to learn how to babble. And here's more...(Draws out a book.) Look, an English textbook. She's a real brainwashed oralist. OK, I think that's all.

FIRST DOCTOR Let me see. (FIRST DOCTOR plunges his arm deeply into the opened stomach, and a hand, which is really SECOND DOCTOR'S hand, appears out of PATIENT'S mouth. SECOND DOCTOR bites the hand and FIRST DOCTOR withdraws his arm/hand with a scream.)

FIRST DOCTOR Ouch! OK, that's all. Finished. No more. (To NURSE.) Give me a needle and thread. The green thread.

SECOND DOCTOR (To FIRST DOCTOR.) Pink is better. It matches her skin color.

FIRST DOCTOR OK. Go and get it. Hold it! Now that her belly is empty, we have to put something back inside it. What?

NURSE A TTY? [Note: A teletypewriter, which makes telephone communication accessible for Deaf people.]

FIRST DOCTOR Yeah! That's great. (Inserts it into PATIENT'S stomach.)

SECOND DOCTOR I got an idea! A T-shirt with ABCs in sign on the front! (Inserts it.) Is that all we have to put inside her?

FIRST DOCTOR Here's a book on ASL! ASL is our language

(Inserts it.) Is that all we have to put inside her?

SECOND DOCTOR One more thing we almost forgot. An "I Love You" button. (Inserts it.) [Author's note: One can fingerspell the initial letters, I, L, and Y, simultaneously on one hand. This configuration is often represented on pins, buttons, posters, and so forth as an acceptance of deaf people, their disability, and their unique mode of communication.]

(BOTH DOCTORS exchange glances and agree that this is all. NURSE gives needle and thread to FIRST DOCTOR, and he sews up the wound with big spiral motions. He asks NURSE for scissors, and when NURSE is slow, he bites off the thread himself. When SECOND DOCTOR removes mask from face, PATIENT springs up and raises her arm in Deaf Power salute.)

MRS. GREENE (To EVERYONE.) Come on. Applaud them. (EVERYONE claps wildly.)

(MRS. GREENE calls directly to the four ACTORS to come to the platform. All bow before the AUDIENCE, including MRS. WISEMAN, who awkwardly moves in front of the others to bow.)

The skit shows images of what Deaf is and what it is not. Prior to the operation the patient was audiologically deaf but not culturally Deaf. The operation removed that which identified her as an oralist. The hearing aid was the first to go. As the authors note, "While a hearing aid is often useful to one whose hearing is impaired, some deaf people who cannot benefit at all from such a device resent the assumption of many hearing people that a hearing aid 'cures' deafness. Such a mistaken assumption not only overestimates the efficacy of hearing aids; it also implies that deafness is an illness or a defect that one ought to get rid of" (Bragg & Bergman 1981).

The patient is also ridiculed as being "dumb." She swallowed the hearing aid thinking that she would be able to hear. For Deaf people, the use of the expression "deaf and dumb" is repugnant. Although on the decline due to the efforts of deaf awareness education and the like, it is a phrase still used in the hearing world. Dumb originally referred to the lack of speech, but it has taken on the meaning of lack of intelligence. The skit plays with this popular usage of the word and with its double meaning. One informant felt that since the patient is an oralist she is more a part of the hearing world. It was felt that this was another play on the expression "deaf and dumb"—that audiologically the patient was deaf, but by not signing and by not being a member of the Deaf community, she was indeed dumb.

After removing some very obvious symbols of the hearing world—a microphone, a portable radio and a loudspeaker—the doctors extract a tongue "that she used to learn to babble." This is the item that clearly labels her an oralist. Images of flapping tongues and babbling mouths to identify oralists are rampant within the folk tradition of Deaf people. For example, the name sign for one prestigious oral institution, the Clark School in Northampton, Massachussets, is a **C** handshape with the base hand mimicking an open mouth while the dominant hand makes a wagging tongue (**U** handshape). Often when telling stories that involve an oralist, Deaf people make exaggerated mouth movements in parody of oral speech.

The final item removed from the patient is the English textbook, which is what indicates that "she's a real brainwashed oralist." Most culturally Deaf Americans are bilingual and are skilled in English as a first or second language. "Most Deaf people take pride in their English skills." However, "it is not proficiency with English that defines you as a Deaf person. It is your skills with ASL that does that." The English textbook is more representative of the hearing world's expectations and measurement of Deaf mastery and a total ignorance of ASL proficiency.

The skit shows us what is not Deaf—hearing aids, microphones, portable radios, loudspeakers, tongues, oralist philosophy and English. The empty patient is filled with examples of things that are Deaf—a TTY, a T-shirt with the ABCs in sign on the front of it, a book on ASL and an "I Love You" button.

The "oralist other" is an out-group within the Deaf world. Deaf people generally tolerate oralists and in some cases view them as benign. There is even an underlying camaraderie between the two groups. Though oral, the oralists are still deaf and have suffered at the hands of the hearing world. At times they are even pitied, perhaps because they are caught in a kind of limbo between two worlds. (The cast of characters in Tales From a Clubroom lists "an ex-oralist who signs awkwardly.") Comments from some informants seem to have this sense of pity. "They seem more isolated, more dependent on the hearing world." "They miss more." "They may be able to speak, but they have nothing to say."

Still, defining oralists as "the other" is a way of defining who the Deaf are not. Thus, oralists often are the object of disparagement humor. The jokes usually center on their speech, their mistakes in speaking, or comic exaggerations of people trying to produce speech or having trouble lipreading. The latter can be seen in the following example.

THREE DEAF ORALISTS

Three deaf oralists met on a train in England. They started a conversation in lip-reading. It went as follows:
A. We're in Wembly.
B. No, it's Thursday.
C. I'm thirsty, too. Let's get a drink.

This joke was collected from a Deaf man who was quite adept with speech himself and had been told to him by others who, like him, have a sense of speech sounds and how they look on the mouth. Interestingly, this is a variation of a American hearing joke that involves three Englishmen and makes fun of British English pronunciation.

Sometimes, however, oralists are not just the object of humor. When they espouse the virtues of oralism or disparage the use of sign or, even, express their shame at being deaf, then they are seen as far from benign. In situations where they are viewed as representing all Deaf people, oralists represent a very real danger because there is the risk that they reinforce in the hearing majority a false or erroneous view of Deaf people.

Even more dangerous in this respect than the oralist other, however, are two other marginal Deaf identities: the "think-hearing" other and the "hard-of-hearing" other.

There is a long history of ill feelings between Deaf and hard-of-hearing people, too long-standing to be dealt with properly here. Suffice it to say, that from a Deaf point of view, hard-of-hearing people have been "speaking for Deaf people," "representing themselves as Deaf people (intentionally or not)," and/or "taking jobs from Deaf people."

It should be noted that there are many culturally Deaf individuals who could be defined audiometrically as hard of hearing, having a dB loss of less than 50 or so. The differentiation between audiometric and attitudinal hard-of-hearing can be seen in the following item of folkspeech:

HARD-OF-HEARING

HARD-OF-HEARING is signed normally as in Figure 18. But when the sign's movement is modulated to a wider arc signed purposefully and is accompanied by a facial expression implying sarcasm, the meaning is a derogatory slur.

HARD-OF-HEARING
Figure 18

It is explained that for someone from the hearing world to refer to a person who is "a little hard of hearing" means that the person has a slight hearing impairment—the more the impairment the closer the person is to being deaf. But when someone from the Deaf world refers to a person as being "a little hard-of-hearing," it can mean that the person is putting on airs, or thinks he is better than Deaf. The more "hard-of-hearing" in this case, the further away the person is from being Deaf (for further discussion see also Padden: 1980).

Another marginal identity within the Deaf world is that which is described in the following popular item of Deaf folk-speech/Blason Populaire—glossed **THINK-HEARING**.

THINK-HEARING is signed by using the handshape, movement and palm orientation of the sign for **HEARING**, Figure 19, but changing the place of articulation to the forehead, where the sign for **THINK**, Figure 20, and other expressions of mental activity are signed.

Figure 19   **Figure 20**
HEARING   **THINK**

This is a good example of how the group maintains acceptable Deaf behavior and enhances the solidarity of the in-group. The sign is used to refer to a Deaf person who appears to be a member of the community, but who thinks more like a hearing person. It is analogous to the expression "Oreo" for a black person who is black on the outside but white on the inside, or the Native American "Apple," or Asian-American "Banana." Like these epithets, it implies not only a split identity but also that the split is between in-group and out-group membership. One appears to be a member of the minority group, but in behavior and spirit identifies more with the oppressor. **THINK-HEARING** people think they are superior to other Deaf people." "They think they represent Deaf people but it's not true." "I suppose some Deaf people have to **THINK-HEARING** to get where they have gotten in their jobs, but the hearing world should not see them as representing Deaf people...but they do."

The oralist other, the HARD-OF-HEARING other and the THINK-HEARING other are all marginal identities. They are part of the Deaf world but their loyalty and sense of self also embrace the hearing world. For the oralist other this identification with the hearing world is almost complete. For the hard-of-hearing and think hearing others, the degree of identification varies and can be context specific: they may be more "hearing" on the job than at home.

These more marginal identities are dangerous for the Deaf world and its continued existence. Deaf people can clearly see where the hearing other stand. They are the oppressor. If they prove themselves attitudinally, they are allowed some measure of membership in the extended Deaf community, as was seen with the Confederate officer in "Sign Language Saves a Life." But with these more marginal identities the situation is not clear. They are Deaf but they are hearing. Further, they reinforce erroneous majority views of Deaf identity. Perhaps this is why there is so much within the folk tradition that mocks the oralist, the hard-of-hearing and the think-hearing elements in the Deaf world. Bascom states that one of the functions of folklore is to maintain conformity to accepted patterns of behavior (1965: 294). The operation skit and the examples of HARD-OF-HEARING and THINK-HEARING act as strong agents to reaffirm what behavior is and is not appropriate for a Deaf person.

These marginal identity groups do the most damage to the Deaf world when the hearing majority mistakenly views them as representative of all Deaf people. The majority may then come to any number of false conclusions: that all Deaf people can speak (or want to speak); that all Deaf people can read lips; that Deaf people can do without interpreters and so on. Perhaps the greatest misconception these groups foster, however, is the notion that deafness, rather than being a difference between people, is a condition that Deaf people want to and can overcome.

Much of the oppression of Deaf people stems from the majority culture not recognizing them as a people. Deaf people are seen as impaired hearing individuals. This pathological view generalizes the hearing impairment over the entire individual producing a majority view of Deaf individuals as handicapped, limited or unable to be fully functioning people.

Interestingly, this situation mirrors that of other minorities. In researching the content of ethnic studies courses across the country, Rose found that the majority "seem to interpret most things from the perspective Schermerhorn once labeled 'victimology'— the view that each and every experience must be seen in terms of deprivation, suffering, and attendant social pathologies; that all known as 'minorities' are, somehow, rather pathetic specimens to be pitied and cared for. (The implication, of course, that the resolution of the problem is to facilitate assimilation)" (1981: 212). This victimological view of minorities strongly parallels the larger society's traditional view of the Deaf community. It is particularly true today when the trend within the deaf educational establishment is away from the residential school and toward "mainstreaming" the Deaf child in the public school setting. As was discussed in Chapter One, the residential school is the primary locus of the linguistic community and the culture of Deaf people. Mainstreaming is perhaps the greatest threat that faces Deaf people and their culture. Now more than ever, it is paramount to maintain the Deaf identity.

How Deaf people feel about this trend can be quickly seen in the following play on the sign for "mainstreaming."

MAINSTREAMING/HYPOCRISY

The play is a blending of the signs for MAINSTREAMING (Figure 21) and HYPOCRISY (Figure 22). MAINSTREAMING is signed in the citation form for it with the /B/ initialized handshape. However, by bending the handshape to a bent /B/ you conclude the movement with the sign for HYPOCRISY. A variation on this is where MAINSTREAMING is signed with an initialized M and the M handshape is bent.

Figure 21
MAINSTREAMING

Figure 22
HYPOCRISY

Another variation on this same theme uses the classifier for INDIVIDUAL PERSON and the sign for OPPRESS. The majority society viewing Deaf people in a pathological or victimological way has led to a situation in which the majority decides what is best for the minority out of ignorance and benevolent paternalism. At best, this results in frustrating interaction between majority and minority; at worst, such misguided efforts could bring about the ethnocide of Deaf people. In the face of this adversity, it is critical for the group to reaffirm and maintain its identity. Individuals who may fit the majority view of deaf people are viewed as a threat to the group's survival.

So it is that we find folk traditions whose effects are to reaffirm Deaf identity and define what is not Deaf. When these traditions take the form of disparagement humor—aimed at either the oppressor majority or the marginal groups whose actions can perpetuate oppression—they can serve as buffers against the oppression and injustices suffered by the group. (It is ironic, though, that the operation skit makes use of the same sort of pathological view that is criticized when employed by the majority. In it, the "impaired" Deaf person is "fixed" by being made less oral, much the way the majority often thinks the Deaf person could be fixed by being made more oral.)

An illustration of disparagement humor aimed at the hearing majority can be seen in the following anecdote:

CAN YOU READ?

You know this really happened to a friend of mine. He was at this bar and some hearing person handed him a note and it said, "Can you read?" My friend wrote back, "No, but I can write." The hearing guy said, oh, and believed him.

The Deaf American folk tradition has a wealth of in-group humor surrounding in-group/out-group points of conflict, frustration and/or repression. The above anecdote and variations have been collected in California; Washington, D. C.; New York and Massachusetts. Sometimes it is told as having happened to the person telling it; sometimes to a friend. Either way, this story has a wide distribution and is told again and again to a receptive audience. It paints a picture of a rather ignorant hearing person who is typical of many whom Deaf people encounter. They are so smart and know so much better than Deaf people, but pass a note that says, "Can you read?" "Who's dumb now?" one informant remarked. Or they speak in a loud pejorative manner as if they were talking to a child—similar to how some Americans behave toward people who do not speak English.

Being patronized by someone who is ignorant is not an uncommon experience for Deaf people, and the irony of that situation is not lost on them. The following is another anecdote that is told as being true, actually happening to the teller or a friend.

BAR CHAT

One time when I was at this bar, there was a hearing fellow sitting next to me. He tried to talk with me, I pointed to my ears and shook my head, indicating that I was Deaf. That didn't bother him really, he took out a pen and started to write to me on the napkin. We were chatting writing back and forth for a while, when another hearing guy came and sat on the other side of me and began writing too. The three of us just sat there drinking and writing and writing and writing.

After a while I went to the men's room. When I came back it was the
funniest sight. They were sitting there at the bar still writing back and
forth to each other—two hearing guys, imagine! I went home and I
imagine that they could be sitting there still writing notes to each
other.

While not as disparaging as "Can you read?" this anecdote is
reflective of a common interaction with the hearing world for Deaf
people: the hearing person thinks he is being nice or helping the
Deaf person, when in fact he may be creating a situation that is
maintained by the Deaf person out of politeness. How do you tell
someone who is sure you need their help and is being noble to
give it that in fact you really don't need them? Or worse, that their
"help" is actually causing more of a problem? The informant said,
"They were nice enough guys, but it sure is a lot of work to have
a bar chat in writing." I asked, "It seems that they thought they
were being nice to you and you were actually trying not to hurt
their feelings. Is that right?" "Yes, exactly!" was the reply.

Within recent years there have been sign language texts and
curriculum developed to teach ASL. This movement has pro-
duced a veritable explosion in the numbers of hearing people
learning to sign. This influx of outsiders becoming privy to the one
major identifying characteristic of Deaf people is seen by the community as a mixed blessing. For some it is seen as a way for more
access to the hearing world, if "they" become sign skilled. It may
mean more interpreters will be available. It could mean that Deaf
children would have more sign skilled teachers, and that communication between hearing parents and their Deaf children could
improve. However, some Deaf folks see this as intrusive. That this
situation is a source of anxiety or hostility, I think, can be seen in
the following riddle and joking behaviors that tease and make fun
of the signing skills of hearing people.

SIGN LANGUAGE RIDDLE

What is the sign for **CHEST-OF-DRAWERS**?

| **Figure 23** | **Figure 24** |
| DRAWER | LAY (INTERCOURSE) |

As figures 23 and 24 show, the sign for DRAWER and LAY (INTERCOURSE) are similar. The signs themselves differ primarily in the handshape parameter, facial expression and intensity of the manner they are signed.

To sign CHEST-OF-DRAWERS involves the pluralizing of the sign for DRAWER, which is done in this case by reduplicating the sign. This replicating process of the sign for DRAWER can easily have the appearance of the repeated intensity that one might find when signing LAY (INTERCOURSE). This would be especially so for a new signer who has not yet mastered a competency of nuance and subtlety of facial expression and movement in the language.

To date, I have only see this riddle in a Deaf/hearing context with the Deaf person asking the hearing person. Where the riddler is a hearing person, it has been collected only in the context of a sign language class or in a social group associated with sign language learning.

Another instance of teasing/mocking a hearing signer is seen in the following anecdote told by a Deaf sign language teacher.

PETER

Well, you know how some hearing students make up name signs.
This kid that was in my class was big-headed. He thought he knew it
all about signing. Then he showed me his name sign—(which was)
"P" on the nose. I just smiled and said nothing.

Figure 25
PEE

"P" on the nose is the sign for **PEE** as illustrated in Figures 25
or, depending on the movement, it could also be the sign for
PENIS. Either way is it a source of humor for the Deaf teacher and
those she told. The custom of giving a name sign is one that is
strictly Deaf. A name sign is a major identity symbol of Deaf
people (for further discussion see Supalla 1992, 1986; Meadows
1977; and elsewhere in this chapter). Hearing people can have
name signs but the name signs are generally given to them by a
Deaf person. A hearing person who uses a self-created name sign
could be an innocent victim of simply not knowing the finer
points of the custom. He could also be seen as demonstrating a
clear disregard and disrespect for the culture of Deaf people. And
since the latter is a more commonplace in the Deaf experience, it
is no doubt that this is a source for the humor in this story. Of
course, there is an outside chance that Peter has been given his
name sign intentionally by a Deaf person. Either way, his name
sign clearly demonstrates his distance from the in-group, and by

not correcting it, the Deaf teacher reinforces and maintains that distance.

Another instance involves the sign for I-LOVE-YOU, or ILY as it is also referred to. This sign had its origin in the residential school. As illustrated in Figure 26 it is the combination of I, L and Y handshapes signed simultaneously. It was a sign that was intensely private and used only by school sweethearts to each other in secret.

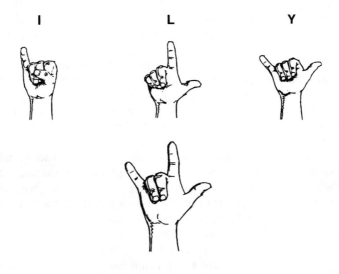

| I | L | Y |

Figure 26   Illustration by Frank Allen Paul
ILY

Since the 1960s, the sign has come into popular usage and is now heavily used as a greeting, a farewell, a logo meaning "I love deaf children" or "I love sign language." It is printed on T-shirts, bumper stickers and stationery. It is fashioned into jewelry, sculpture and needlepoint.

There is a parody of the use of ILY found among Deaf community members. ILY might be signed in mocking imitation of a hearing signer. A text of a playful one-hand-shape conversation that I collected was done entirely with ILY handshapes. Informant interviews all pointed to the origin of the sign, how it would never be

used the way it is now, and all felt that the wholesale commercial-
ization of ILY was largely done by the hearing world and was of-
fensive. For some who saw it as a genuine attempt on the part of
hearing people in the support of Deaf children it was somewhat
excusable and tolerated. It is now in fairly common usage by both
hearing and Deaf people.

These riddles, anecdotes, teasing behaviors and parodies continue to be told as they provide an outlet for the frustrations of everyday interaction and anxieties of coping with the hearing world.
With a clear portrait of who "we" are and who "they" are, they
also serve as a point of reaffirmation of what it is to be Deaf while
strengthening the bond felt by the group who shares this experience.

So far we have been examining the Deaf identity in juxtaposition to that which is not Deaf. As in any cultural group there are a
myriad of identities within the group—sex, race, religion, status,
geographical region, occupation, etc. As we can see in the diversity of characters for *Tales From A Clubroom* the Deaf community is
no exception.

As we have discussed earlier, the name sign is a traditional
and important identity symbol for Deaf people. It is a formalized
gesture which refers to an individual or a place. The assigning of
a name sign to an individual in the Deaf community is somewhat
unusual because of who performs the task. In the hearing world,
names are conferred upon children by parents. In the Deaf community this is true for Deaf families, but for the majority of Deaf
children, their name signs are more often assigned by the peer
group. Supalla divides name signs into two categories, those that
are descriptive and those that are arbitrary (1986). Arbitrary name
signs are generally the handshape of the person's initial(s) signed
in neutral space or on a specific part of the body. For example on
the chin. It is not uncommon to find that Deaf families have a family tradition of placing the name sign in the same location so that
each family member may have a different initial but all are signed
in the identical place.

The process of creating the descriptive name sign is one that
involves the person's initial(s) combined with the place of articulation and movement in such a way as to capture some personal
characteristic of the person. For example, the descriptive name

signs for Presidents Carter and Nixon, Figures 27 and 28.

/C/ handshape incor-
porating the sign for
NUT (PEANUT)

Figure 27
PRESIDENT-CARTER

/N/ handshape
incorporating the
sign for **LIAR**

Figure 28
PRESIDENT-NIXON

Place name signs on the surface do not seem to have the intimacy and link to identity that personal name signs have. Often
they are simply fingerspelled initials: KC for Kansas City or LA for
Los Angeles. In the case of short names—Ohio, Iowa—the place
name is often fingerspelled in its entirety. (In some cases a place
name will have a distinct sign: the sign for CALIFORNIA is the
same as the sign for GOLD).

Within the Deaf world a large measure of identity is tied to where you are from—the understood question being asked is really "Which residential school did you attend?" This importance of place can be seen in customary introductions where the order of biographical information exhanged is usually name first, where from second. Whereas, American hearing people in similar circumstance would more typically identify their occupation. In this light we can see that place names for particular cities and states become more personal for the Deaf individual because of this tie with the names of the residential schools. Informants say that the feeling for these schools goes beyond school pride. The schools are viewed more as "home" by many Deaf individuals. For some it is with great ambivalence because their memories of their school experience were harsh. Since residential school attendance is such a shared experience throughout the national Deaf community, the place name of one's school, often the same as one's home city or state, becomes easily linked with one's own identity as a distinguishing characteristic. Thus, place name signs are just as ripe a target for teasing as personal name signs.

In the course of my collecting of slurs[7] on place name signs, informants more often than not expressed that if I really wanted to collect such things I should go to Gallaudet University, as that is where many of them were learned. Since 1864 Gallaudet has been the world's only liberal arts college for Deaf people. The students at Gallaudet represent their respective localities in the national community. Since, "teasing tends to deny distance and to symbolize a potential closeness..."(Howell, 1973: 6) it stands to reason that we would find this student community a rich source of slurred place names. The following examples incorporate a variety of forms, both fingerspelling mime and slurs of individual signs are used.[7]

The following examples slurring Texas show a one handed fingerspelling of T-E-X-A-S with an obscene sign interjected for the letter X and a two handed version. Interestingly these two versions are nearly identical in meaning.

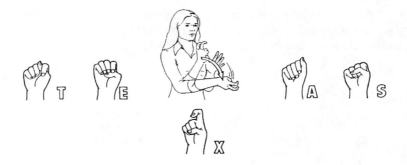

Figure 29
PROMISCUOUS-PERSON
(can be either male or female)

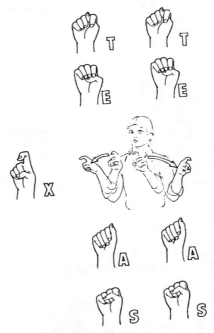

Figure 30
PROMISCUOUS-WOMAN

Another example is one that an informant particularly liked because it looked so silly—a slur on the name sign for West Virginia, which is ordinarily fingerspelled W-V-A.

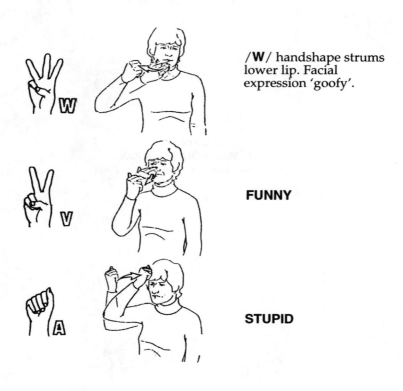

/**W**/ handshape strums lower lip. Facial expression 'goofy'.

FUNNY

STUPID

Figure 31
WEST-VIRGINIA

The following example (Figure 32) slurs North Carolina with an **N** and a **C** being signed on the nose to give the impression of a large, ugly nose.

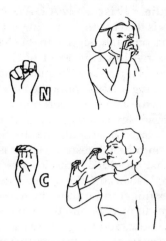

Figure 32
NORTH-CAROLINA

Another technique is the incorporation of a name sign with a derogatory gesture such as thumbing the nose, thumbs down, or giving someone the finger, such as:

The sign for California when the handshape and palm orientation of the final movement are changed to the universal gesture of "thumbs down."

Figure 33
CALIFORNIA

Another example of this is a slur on the name sign for Alabama, which ordinarily is merely **A-L-A** fingerspelled. The place of ᴀqrticulation, as is the case for most fingerspelled name signs, is in neutral space in front of the signer. In the slurred version, the place of articulation for **A-L-A** is in front of the face. with the thumb touching the nose. Thus, when the place name is signed it is simultaneously producing a "thumbing the nose" gesture.

The same is true in a very commonly found slur for Los Angeles, whose name sign is a fingerspelled **L-A**. Again, the repositioning of the place of articulation to the nose produces the simultaneous "thumbing" gesture. There is a variant slur for Los Angeles which has an added wrinkle—one I have not seen in slurs for Alabama. In this variant, the signer substitutes the middle finger for the index finger in forming the manual letter **L**. The resulting slur manages to incorporate the name sign for Los Angeles, a thumbing of the nose, and the gesture for "giving the finger."

The last two examples are frequently found in common usage. They both involve simple parameter substitutions.

Name sign   Slurred Name Sign

Figure 34
NEW YORK

The change in palm orientation implies 'underhanded,''-seamy,' 'the dark side.' This can also imply 'dirty.

Figure 35
BUFFALO, N.Y.

The sign for **BUFFALO, N.Y.** is the same as that for the animal. It is slurred when the place of articulation is changed from the forehead to the signer's armpit. The city has been know to be called the "armpit of New York State."

There is a further factor contributing to the use of teasing behaviors at Gallaudet and it concerns the age of the participants. The average student age at entry to Gallaudet is approximately 19. These students are the elite of the Deaf community—a community which has a 95% endogamous marriage rate. Given this tradition and the ages of the individuals, it is reasonable to conclude that this teasing behavior is also related to mate selection and sexual exploration. The explicit content of the majority of texts is overtly sexual. And, as Howell points out, the more likely the potential relationship the more likely that teasing will occur (1973: 15).

Another tradition at Gallaudet that relates to identity is the "Rat Funeral," which is a ritual marking the end of the prefreshman or preparatory year and the beginning of one's freshman status.

THE RAT FUNERAL

I'll be telling you about the Gallaudet University tradition of the Rat Funeral. Initially it was done by Gallaudet's pre-freshman students. During my time by the freshman. Well now it has returned to the prep students. Anyway, I'll tell you my experience. During the first two weeks of the school year we would go through hazing. And just before the last day we would chose someone to buy a rat and bring it back to school. All the guys would gather outside and single out the person who was most squeamish. This part of the activity was an all boys thing. Well, first we would make him play with the rat, and then later make him kill it. All the guys would stand around egging him on until finally he would squish the rat. The next day we would prepare for the funeral. We would make a coffin, paint it and decorate it nicely. Then we would lay the rat in it and close the casket. Now the same night all the boys and girls would dress in appropriate funeral attire—black ties, dresses and we would smear Vicks Vaporub under our eyes to make ourselves cry. Then we would line up for the funeral procession. It was mandatory to cry and mourn to lament the end of our prep year. That's where it came from, the R-A-T in the word preparatory. The sign used for freshman is also the sign for `RAT.' The ceremony symbolized our last year as prep students. We would all now be official Gallaudet University students. So, we would march to the gravesite and when the eulogy was complete, we would bury the rat.

The Deaf identity, like any other, is multiple in nature. Deaf Americans see themselves as a part of the Deaf world, but also see themselves as a part of the larger American society as well. That the Deaf individual feels invisible in this larger world, I think, is evidenced by another major theme found within the folklore what can be categorized as—"Deaf Can." Images of "Deaf can" are many. Stories of Deaf contributions to society or the worth of Deaf people are told again and again. Such as the introduction of the baseball umpire's gesturing system for balls and strikes which is attributed to William "Dummy" Hoy who played with the Cinncinatti Red Stockings in the late 1800s. He was unable to hear the umpire's calls and suggested a system that he could see. Another sports related contribution is seen in the story of the origin of the football huddle. There is more variety in the specifics of how this came about than in the "Dummy Hoy" legend, but details usually center on the formidable Gallaudet team that was widely respected and played other local teams such as the Naval Academy and the University of Virginia in addition to other Deaf teams. The huddle was just a natural evolution of Deaf football teams especially if playing against another Deaf team and not wanting to reveal one's signals. If a specific name is credited it is that of Paul Hubbard the 1892 quarterback. These are particularly enjoyable texts since the sports world is one that is very important to the Deaf community.

The material culture, too, is full of items that reaffirm the idea that "Deaf can." Deaf people can do for themselves and adapt to living in a hearing world with things such as door-knocking devices that shake the room rather than just make a sound, as follows:

THE CANNONBALL DOOR KNOCKER

A cannon ball was tied to a rope. The rope them was strung through a hook in the ceiling and then through a hole in the door. Someone who came to the door and wanted to get the attention of the Deaf occupant would just pull the rope in and out and the cannon ball would hit the floor up and down making the floor vibrate. The Deaf person inside the house would feel the vibrations in the floor and know that someone was at the door.

Another strategy is as follows:

STRING ON A CHAIR

A string or rope would be tied to a chair and the chair placed in the middle of the room. The string was then strung through the keyhole of the door. When someone came to the door, they could pull the string, which would knock over the chair and the Deaf person inside would know someone was at the door. Of course, this meant that the Deaf person had to be in the room. It was useful in hotels.

Other strategies, also reported as useful in hotels, are blowing smoke through the keyhole or slipping a piece of paper under the door and wiggling it back and forth hoping to attract attention.

Alarm clocks are another source of inventiveness, as we can see in the following:

EARLY ALARM CLOCKS

There was one boy who was at the school where I taught, who made clocks for Deaf people of the area. Not just any clock, alarm clocks. These clocks worked like this: On the shelf over your bed would be a wind up clock. Under the shelf would be two slats of wood hinged together. Sort of like a draw bridge. The outer board had a hook that latched onto the key of the clock. And on that board would be a piece of lead to make it heavy. When the alarm went off, that board would become unhooked and hit the bed. Let me tell you, it hit with such a bang it shook us right out of bed. That's how I woke up for many years until I got my radio clock.

On this same theme, this informant continued with the following tall tale about a Deaf Miner.

THE DEAF MINER

There was this Deaf man in Montana who worked in the mines. He used to use an old flat iron to wake up every morning. That was his alarm clock. I don't know how exactly, but somehow he rigged it up so that the iron was suspended from the ceiling from a string that was attached to a wind up clock. So that when the alarm would go off, it would release the string and the iron would then hit the floor with such a force that it shook the whole house. All the neighbors for miles around relied on that flat iron dropping to get them out of bed every morning. Well, one day the man got married. He and his bride went away on their honeymoon and were gone for three days. When they came back home, lo and behold they had found that no one had worked the mines for three days. The whole town was still asleep just waiting for that flat iron to drop!

This fanciful text nicely illustrates not only the Deaf person's independence, capabilities and desire to be a part of the hearing world, but also the hearing community's dependence upon the capable Deaf individual.

Bauman asserts, "Folklore is a function of shared identity." In this chapter we have seen but a few samples of the folk tradition of Deaf people. Through this folklore we have seen instances of how Deaf identity is formed, maintained and strengthened. We have seen images of self-sameness bound by the language and cultural experience. We have seen a Deaf continuity with a Deaf past through historic references and Deaf heroes who have gone before. We have seen how the group defines itself in terms of who they are and in terms of who they are not—by defining "the other." There is no Deaf world without the hearing world and likewise there is no hearing world as such without reference to the Deaf world. We have also seen that within the Deaf world there are further definitions of what Deaf is by establishing the "oralist," "hard-of-hearing" and "think-hearing" others. And further, that within that world the Deaf identity is multiple in nature.

Deaf identity serves as a core for Deaf individuals. In a world that often views Deaf people as handicapped, it is the one thing through which they can see themselves as whole and fully functioning human beings— perfectly fine Deaf people. To lose it would relegate Deaf people to an identity formed for them by the majority world—that of a "broken" or impaired hearing person.

---

[7] As is often the case with slurring, many if not the majority of slurred name signs are obscene in nature. For further examples, the reader is referred to the original publication of this dissertation (available from University Microfilms and/or Rutherford).

CHAPTER VI

CONCLUSION

Observations and Analyses

The American Deaf community has a rich folkloristic tradition, which serves American Deaf people the same as any folk group's traditions do. It entertains and amuses, educates and builds competencies, establishes and maintains identity, validates and regulates conformity of the group.

There is perhaps no better way to learn about a people than through a study of their folklore. An examination of Deaf American folk traditions does this and further provides us with a clear illustration of the nature of culture as a mechanism by which a people adapt to their environment.

As we have discussed earlier, the environment that Deaf Americans find themselves in is one of a minority culture within a majority world that for the most part does not recognize Deaf people as a cultural group, but rather views them as isolated hearing impaired individuals. Their language is not recognized as bona fide. It is seen as a substandard form of communication, of little value, and its use is discouraged. Particularly oppressive is the situation in which the majority culture—out of ignorance—denies the formal recognition of a "home" language and culture of Deaf people and at the same time controls the self-determination of Deaf individuals. A dominant culture may look at any minority culture's language with a jaundiced eye, but it is rare that we find a majority believing that the language and culture of a people didn't even exist.

The most salient adaptive mechanism created by the culture of Deaf Americans is obviously their language—a visual language for a people who perceive the world in visual terms. The relationship between language and identity for the Deaf individual is profound. The use of ASL is the single most identifying characteristic of membership in the Deaf community, it is that which establishes the individual's Deaf identity. This is reflected throughout the folklore. Deaf characters sign. The two Deaf soldiers in the Civil War legend identify each other by signing **YOU DEAF? SAME-AS-ME,** not by saying **YOU CAN'T HEAR EITHER?** The Deaf identification as reflected in the folklore is with the language and is in terms of what the people are—Deaf—and not in terms of what they are not—impaired.

The establishment and maintenance of a group's identity are important functions of folk traditions. This is especially true for a minority culture, and for the Deaf world it is critical. The Deaf cultural identity offers the Deaf individual the opportunity to be a fully functioning whole person. It provides membership in a group of self-same individuals with a heritage and tradition well connected to the past. This grounding in a Deaf identity then permits Deaf individuals to know who they are and enables the development of positive self-esteem. These are requisite for learning and functioning as a productive member of society. From this base the Deaf individual can best learn, develop skills and integrate into the majority world. It is ironic that the majority society also holds these as goals for Deaf people, but generally fails to recognize the tool—culture—that would best help Deaf people to achieve them.

The maintenance of the Deaf identity is a major force found in Deaf folklore. There is a virtual font of in-group/out-group jokes, legends and anecdotes that establish the majority world of hearing society as "the Other" and that solidify the Deaf group. "Folklore furnishes a socially sanctioned outlet for cultural pressure points and individual anxieties" (Dundes, 1980: 36). So it is not surprising that since the recent takeover by the University of California of the neighboring property long-occupied by the California School for the Deaf, we have seen a resurgence of the legend of how in the late 1800s, after playing against the Deaf School, the Cal football team stole the CSD symbol—the Bear—and made it their team mascot. It was taken as if anything associated with the Deaf school was fair game. The takeover of the CSD property, a school that predates the university, was viewed much the same way as the mascot incident by the Deaf community. "The other," in this case the university, hasn't changed much in the eyes of Deaf folks. The telling of the legend reaffirms that fact.

Further, folklore "offers an escape from the everyday hardships, inequities and injustices found by the group (Bascom, 1965: 285). Laughing at the ignorance of a "hearing other" who passes a Deaf person a note asking if he can read assuages some of the daily frustration of dealing with a majority culture that holds on to its stereotypes and prejudices about Deaf people. Such stories reaffirm the group by illustrating clearly who they are not.

The Deaf identity is also reaffirmed through creative sign play and storytelling performance. When a people use their language creatively, it reflects an attitude that the language is indeed worthwhile. The performer and the audience have an awareness of the creative potential of the language. The creative play in ASL demonstrates a positive attitude toward selves—be it the cleverness of an ABC story skillfully told or a story of "How Sign Language Saved a Life."

Another adaptive function served by the folk tradition is seen in educational strategies that help build skills and competencies. Word and sign games foster linguistic competencies; spelling strategies (Padden, 1985) assist in acquiring English proficiency; group storytelling play develops narrative mastery; and bilingual play assists in the development of proficiency in both languages of the Deaf community—ASL and English. There is also a propensity, which in folkloristic terms is perhaps custom, toward facilitating communication and making sure all in the group have understood what information may have been shared. There is a great tendency toward teaching each other. There is a very high value placed on information and an equally high value on being sure the information is shared.

It is the folk traditions of the community that establish and maintain the Deaf identity, that provide key adaptive strategies for the Deaf individual to live in a hearing world, and that give strength to overcome the harshness and inequities suffered by an oppressed people. It is the folklore that validates the culture and thereby validates the individual. In his 1913 speech "The Preservation of Sign Language," George Veditz asserted, "As long as we have Deaf people on earth, we will have sign language." His is a promising and hopeful note, but it is predicated on the existence of Deaf people on earth. It should be added that we will have Deaf people on earth as long as they have their folk traditions.

REFERENCES

Akerly, S. 1824. Observations on the Language of Signs. *Journal Science and Arts.* 8:348-358.

Andersson, Yerker. 1975. The Deaf as a Subculture. *An Orientation to Deafness for Social Workers: Papers from the Conference March 18-20.* Washington, D.C.: Gallaudet College Public Service Programs

Avedon, Elliott M. and Brian Sutton-Smith. 1971. *The Study of Games.* New York: J. Wiley.

Babcock-Abrahams, Barbara 1975. *The Reversible World: Essays in Symbolic Inversion.* Ithaca, New York: Cornell University Press. 13-36.

Bahan, Ben and Sam Supalla. 1991. *American Sign Language Literature Series.* San Diego: Dawn Sign Press.

Baker, Charlotte. 1977. Regulators and Turn-Taking in American Sign Language Discourse. In Lynn Friedman, ed. *On The Other Hand: New Perspectives on American Sign Language.* New York: Academic Press. 215-236.

_____ and Carol Padden. 1978. *American Sign Language: A Look At Its History, Structure, and Community.* Silver Spring, MD: T.J. Publishers, Inc.

_____ and Robin Battison, Eds. 1980. *Sign Language and the Deaf Community: Essays in Honor of William C. Stokoe.* Silver Spring, MD: National Association of the Deaf.

Barron, Milton L. 1950. A Content Analysis of Inter-group Humor. *American Sociological Review.* 15:88-94.

Barth, Fredrik. 1969. *Ethnic Groups and Boundaries.* Boston: Little, Brown.

Bascom, William R. 1965a. Folklore and Anthropology. in Alan Dundes, ed. *The Study of Folklore.* Englewood Cliffs: Prentice-Hall 25-33.

_____. 1965b Four Functions of Folklore. in Alan Dundes, ed. *The Study of Folklore*. Englewood Cliffs: Prentice-Hall 279-298.

_____. 1965c The Forms of Folklore: Prose Narrative. *Journal of American Folklore* 78:3-20.

Basso, Keith. 1979. *Portraits of "The White Man"*. Cambridge: Cambridge University Press.

Bateson, Gregory. 1972. A Theory of Play and Fantasy. In *Steps to an Ecology of Mind*. New York: Ballantine Books 397-524.

Battison, Robin. 1978. *Lexical Borrowing in American Sign Language*. Silver Spring, MD: Linstok Press.

Bauman, Richard. 1971. Differential Identity and the Social Base of Folklore. *Journal of American Folklore* 85:31-41.

_____. 1977. *Verbal Art as Performance*. Rowley, MA: Newbury House.

_____. 1983. The Field Study of Folklore in Context. In *Handbook of American Folklore*. Richard M. Dorson ed. Bloomington, ID: Indiana University Press.

_____ and Joel Sherzer eds. 1974 *Explorations in the Ethnography of Speaking*. London: Cambridge University Press.

Becker, Gaylene. 1981. *Growing Old in Silence*. Berkeley: University of California Press.

Bell, Alexander Graham. 1883. Upon the Formation of a Deaf Variety of the Human Race, paper presented to the National Academy of Science.

Bellugi, Ursula. 1976. Attitudes Toward Sign Language. In *Proceedings of the Seventh World Congress of the World Federation of the Deaf*. A. & F. Crammatte eds. Silver Spring, MD: National Association of the Deaf.

_____. 1972. Studies in Sign Language. In *Psycholinguistics and Total Communication: The State of the Art*. T. J. O'Rourke ed. Washington: *American Annals of the Deaf* 68-84.

_____ and Susan Fischer. 1972. A Comparison of Sign Language and Spoken Language. *Cognition* 1:173-200.

_____ and Edward Klima. 1975. Aspects of Sign Language and Its Structure. In *The Role of Speech in Language*, Kavanagh and Cutting eds. Cambridge: MIT Press 171-205.

Bender, Ruth. 1970. *The Conquest of Deafness: A History of the Long Struggle to Make Possible Normal Living to Those Handicapped by Lack of Normal Hearing*. Cleveland: Case Western Reserve University Press.

Berger, Arthur Asa. 1976. Anatomy of a Joke. In Laughing Matter? A Symposium of Studies on Humor as Communication. *Journal of Communication*, 26, 3:113-115.

Bergson, Henry. 1911. *Laughter: An Essay on the Meaning of the Comic.* Translated by C. Brereton and F. Rothwell. New York: Macmillan.

Best, Harry. 1943. *Deafness and the Deaf in the United States.* New York: Macmillan.

Bettelheim, Bruno. 1972. Play and Education. *School Review* 81:1-13.

Blauner, Robert. 1972. *Racial Oppression in America.* New York: Harper & Row.

Botvin, Gilbert. 1977. A Proppian Analysis of Children's Fantasy Narratives. In P. Stevens ed. *Studies in the Anthropology of Play.* Cornwall, NY: Leisure Press 145-54.

Bower, Eli. 1966. The Achievement of Competency. *Learning and Mental Health in the School.* Washington, D.C.: United States Department of Health, Education and Welfare.

Bragg, Bernard and Eugene Bergman. 1981. *Tales from a Clubroom.* Washington, D.C.: Gallaudet College Press.

Brewster, Paul G. 1953. *American Nonsinging Games.* Norman: University of Oaklahoma.

Bruner, J., J. Allison, and K. Sylva eds. 1976. *Play: Its Role in Development and Evolution,* New York: Basic Books.

Brunvand, Jan Harold. 1968. *The Study of American Folklore.* New York: W.W. Norton & Co..

Burma, John H. 1946. Humor as a Technique in Race Conflict. *American Sociological Review.* 11:710-715.

Caillois, Roger. 1961. *Man, Play and Games.* New York: The Free Press of Glencoe, Inc., Crowell-Collier Publishing.

Charrow, Veda. 1976. A Psycholinguistic Analysis of Deaf English. *Sign Language Studies* 7:139-150.

Cicourel, Aaron. 1978. Sociolinguistic Aspects of the Use of Sign Language. In *Sign Language of the Deaf: Psychological, Linguistic, and Sociological Perspectives,* I.M. Schlesinger and Lila Namir eds. New York: Academic Press 271-314.

_____ and R. Boese. 1972. Sign Language Acquisition and the Teaching of Deaf Children. In *The Functions of Language: An*

Anthropological and Psychological Approach, D. Hymes, C. Cazden and V. John eds. New York: Teachers College Press.

Cochrane, W.   1877.   Methodical Signs Instead of Colloquial. *American Annals of the Deaf* 16:11-17.

Cokely, Dennis. 1980. Sign Language: Teaching, Interpreting, and Educational Policy. In *Sign Language and the Deaf Community* Baker and Battison eds. Silver Spring, MD: National Association of the Deaf.

_____ and Charlotte Baker. 1980. *American Sign Language: A Teacher's Resource Text on Curriculum, Methods and Evaluation.* Silver Spring, MD: T. J. Publishers, Inc.

Conklin, H.D. 1959. Linguistic Play in Its Cultural Context. *Language* 35:631-636.

Cooley, Charles H. 1964. *Human Nature and the Social Order.* New York: Schocken Books, first published in 1902.

Croneberg, Carl. 1965. The Linguistic Community. In Stokoe, Casterline and Croneberg. *A Dictionary of American Sign Language.* Washington, D.C.: Gallaudet College Press.

DeLevita, David J. 1965. *The Concept of Identity.* New York: Basic Books.

DeSantis, Susan. 1976. The Deaf Community in the United States. Working Paper, Linguistics Research Lab, Gallaudet College, Washington, D.C.

DuChamp, M. 1877. The National Institution for the Deaf and Dumb at Paris. *American Annals of the Deaf* 22:1-10.

DeVos, George and Lola Romanucci-Ross eds. 1982. *Ethnic Identity: Cultural Continuities and Change.* Chicago: University of Chicago Press.

Dorson, Richard. 1983. *Handbook of American Folklore.* Bloomington: Indiana University Press.

Douglas, Mary. 1968. The Social Control of Cognition: Some Factors in Joke Perception. *Man* 3:361-76.

Dundes, Alan. 1964. Texture, Text and Context. *Southern Folklore Quarterly* 28:251-65.

_____. 1965. *The Study of Folklore.* Englewood Cliffs: Prentice-Hall. Inc.

_____. 1973. *Mother Wit from the Laughing Barrel: Readings in the Interpretation of Afro-American Folklore.* Englewood Cliffs: Prentice-Hall, Inc.

_____. 1975. *Analytic Essays in Folklore*. The Hague: Mouton.

_____. 1980. *Interpreting Folklore*. Bloomington: Indiana University Press.

_____. 1983. Defining Identity through Folklore. In Anita Jacobson-Widding ed. *Identity: Personal and Socio-Cultural, A Symposium. Uppsala: Studies in Cultural Anthropology* 5: 235-261.

Eastman, Gilbert. 1974. *Sign Me Alice*. Washington, D.C.: Gallaudet College Press.

Eissler, K. 1958. Problems in Identity. *Journal of American Psychoanalytical Association*, 131-142.

Erikson, Erik. 1963. *Childhood and Society.* 2nd rev. ed. New York: W. W. Norton & Co.

Erting, Carol. 1978. Language Policy and Deaf Ethnicity in the United States. *Sign Language Studies*, 19:139-152.

Fant, Louie J., Jr. 1974a. Ameslan: The Communications System of Choice. In Peter J. Fine, ed. *Deafness in Infancy and Early Childhood*. New York: Medcom Press 205-16.

_____. 1974b. *Ameslan: An Introduction to American Sign Language*. Northridge, CA: Joyce Motion Picture Co.

Fay, E. A. 1898. *Marriages of the Deaf in America*. Washington, D.C.: Volta Bureau.

Fay, George. 1882. The Sign Language: The Basis of Instruction for Deaf Mutes. *American Annals of the Deaf* 27:208-211.

Feinberg, Leonard. 1978. The Secret of Humor. *Maledicta* 2:87-110.

Ferguson, Charles. 1959. Diglossia. *Word* 15:325-340.

Fine, Elizabeth. 1984. *The Folklore Text, From Performance to Print*. Bloomington: Indiana University Press.

Fisher, Susan. 1978. Sign Language and Creoles. In Patricia Siple, ed. *Understanding Language Through Sign Language Research*. New York: Academic Press 309-332.

Fishman, Joshua. 1967. Bilingualism With and Without Diglossia; Diglossia With and Without Bilingualism. *Journal of Social Issues* 23:29-38.

Freud, Sigmund. 1916. *Wit and Its Relation to the Unconscious*. London: Fisher and Unwin.

Frishberg, Nancy. 1975. Arbitrariness and Iconicity: Historical Change in American Sign Language. *Language*. 51:696-719.

Fry, William. 1965. *Sweet Madness: A Study of Humor*. Palo Alto, CA: Pacific Books.

Gallaudet, Edward M. 1871. Is the Sign Language Used to Excess in Teaching Deaf-Mutes. *American Annals of the Deaf* 16:26-33.

_____. 1887. The Value of the Sign Language to the Deaf. *American Annals of the Deaf* 32:141-147.

Gannon, Jack. 1980. *Deaf Heritage*. Silver Spring, MD: National Association of the Deaf.

Garvey, Catherine. 1977. *Play.* Cambridge: Harvard University Press.

Geertz, Clifford. *The Interpretation of Cultures*. New York: Basic Books.

_____. 1976. From the Native's Point of View: On the Nature of Anthropological Understanding. In Keith Basso and Henry Selby, eds. *Meaning in Anthropology.* School of American research Advanced Seminar Series. Albuquerque: University of New Mexico Press 221-237.

Glass, R. 1962. Insiders-Outsiders: The Position of Minorities. *New Left Review.* 17:34-45.

Goldstein, Jeffrey H. 1976. Theoretical Notes on Humor. In Laughing Matter? A Symposium of Studies on Humor as Communication. *Journal of Communication.* 26:104-112.

Greenacre, Phyllis. 1958. Early Physical Determinants in the Development of the Sense of Identity. *Journal of the American Psychoanalytic Association* 6:612-627.

Haas, Mary. 1964. Thai Word Games. In Dell Hymes, ed. *Language in Culture and Society: A Reader in Linguistics and Anthropology.* New York: Harper and Row, 301-304.

Hayes, David, Director. 1971. *My Third Eye*. Composition of the cast of the National Theatre of the Deaf. Waterford, CT.

Herskovits, Melville J. 1946. Folklore After a Hundred Years: A Problem in Redefinition. *Journal of American Folklore.* 59:89-107.

Higgins, Paul D. 1980. *Outsiders in a Hearing World*. Beverly Hills: Sage Publications.

_____. 1977. *The Deaf Community: Identity and Interaction in a Hearing World*. Ann Arbor, MI: University Microfilms.

Hillery, George A. 1955. Definitions of Community: Areas of Agreement. *Rural Sociology.* 20:111-123.

Huizinga, Johan. 1955. *Homo Ludens: A Study of the Play Element in Culture*. Boston: Beacon Press.

Humphries, Tom, Carol Padden and T. J. O'Rourke. 1980. *A Basic*

Course in American Sign Language. Silver Spring, MD:T. J. Publishers.

Jacobs, Leo M. 1989. *A Deaf Adult Speaks Out.* Washington, D.C.: Gallaudet University Press.

Jansen, William Hugh. 1959. The Esoteric-Exoteric Factor. *Fabula: Journal of Folktale Studies.* 2:205-211. Reprinted in Alan Dundes, *The Study of Folklore.* 43-51.

Johnson, R.E., Liddell, S., & Erting, C.J. 1989. Unlocking the Curriculum: Principles for Achieving Access in Deaf Education. Gallaudet Research Institute, Working Paper 89-3.

Kannapell, Barbara. 1974. Bilingualism: A New Direction in the Education of the Deaf. *The Deaf American.* 26:9-15.

_____. 1980. Personal Awareness and Advocacy in the Deaf Community. In Baker and Battison, eds. *Sign Language and the Deaf Community: Essays in Honor of William C. Stokoe.* Silver Spring, MD: National Association of the Deaf.

Keep, J. 1871. Natural Signs-Shall They Be Abandoned. *American Annals of the Deaf* 16:17-25.

_____. 1871b. The Sign Language. *American Annals of the Deaf* 16:221-234.

Kimball, Solon T. and James B. Watson, eds. 1972. *Crossing Culture Boundaries.* San Francisco: Chandler.

Kirshenblatt-Gimblett, Barbara. ed. 1976. *Speech Play.* Philadelphia: University of Pennsylvania Press.

_____. 1983. Studying Immigrant and Ethnic Folklore. In Richard M. Dorson, ed. *Handbook of American Folklore.* Bloomington: Indiana University Press. Klima, Edward and Ursula Bellugi. 1979. *The Signs of Language.* Cambridge, MA: Harvard University Press.

_____. 1975. Wit and Poetry in American Sign Language. *Sign Language Studies.* 8:203-224.

Koestler, Arthur. 1964. *The Act of Creation: A Study of the Conscious and Unconscious in Science and Art.* New York: Dell

Labov, William. 1969. The Logic of Non-Standard English. In Aarons, et al. eds. *Linguistic-Cultural Differences and American Education.* Florida Reporter 7

Lambert, Wallace. 1971. A Social Psychology of Bilingualism. In W. H. Whiteley, ed. *Language   Use and Language Change.* London: Oxford University Press, 95-110.

Lane, Harlan. 1992. *The Mask of Benevolence: Disabling of the Deaf Community.* New York: Alfred Knopf.

_____. 1985. *When the Mind Hears.* New York: Random House.

_____. 1977. Notes for a Psycho-History of American Sign Language. *Deaf American.* 30:2-7.

_____ and Francois Grosjean. 1980. *Recent Perspectives on American Sign Language.* Hillsdale, NJ: Lawrence Erlbaum Associates.

Lucas, Ceil and Clayton Valli. 1992. Language Contact in the American Deaf Community. San Diego: Academic Press.

Luckmann, Thomas. 1979. Personal Identity as an Evolutionary and Historical Problem. In von Cranach, Foppa, Lepenies and Ploog, eds. *Human Ethology: Claims and Limits of a New Discipline.* Cambridge: Cambridge University Press, 56-74.

Lunde, A. 1960. The Sociology of the Deaf. In W. Stokoe. *Sign Language Structure: An Outline of Visual Communication Systems of the American Deaf.* University of Buffalo: Occassional Paper 8.

Markowicz, Harry. 1972. Some Sociological Considerations of American Sign Language. *Sign Language Studies.* 1:15-41.

_____. 1974. Is Sign English English? Paper presented at the First Annual Conference on Sign Language. Gallaudet College, Washington, D.C.

_____ and James Woodward. Language and the Maintenance of Ethnic Boundaries in the Deaf Community. *Communication and Cognition.* 11:29-38.

Marshall, H. P. 1961. Relations Between Home Experience and Children's Use of Language in Play Interactions With Peers. *Psychological Monographs.* 75:9-15.

Martineau, William H. 1972. A Model of the Social Functions of Humor. In Goldstein and McGhee, eds. *The Psychology of Humor.* New York: Academic Press.

McDowell, John H. 1983. Children's Folklore. In Richard M. Dorson, ed. *Handbook of American Folklore.* Bloomington: Indiana University Press 314-322.

Mead, George Herbert. 1934. *Mind, Self and Society.* Chicago: University of Chicago Press.

Mead, Margaret. 1968. The Application of Anthropological Techniques to Cross-National Communication. In Alan Dundes, ed.

Every Man His Way. Englewood Cliffs, NJ: Prentice-Hall, 518-536.

Meadows, Katherine. 1972. Sociolinguistics, Sign Language and the Deaf Subculture. In T. J. O'Rourke, ed. *Psycholinguistics and Total Communication: The State of the Art.* Silver Spring, MD: American Annals of the Deaf, 1972.

_____. 1977. Name Signs as Identity Symbols in the Deaf Community. *Sign Language Studies* 17:237-246.

Miller, Ed. 1977. The Use of Sterotypes in Inter-Ethnic Joking as a Means of Communication. *Folklore Annual* 7/8:28-42.

Mindel, Eugene and McCay Vernon. 1971. *They Grow In Silence.* Silver Spring, MD: National Association of the Deaf.

Opie, Iona and Peter. 1959. *The Lore and Language of Schoolchildren.* Oxford: Oxford University Press.

_____. 1969. *Children's Games in Street and Playground.* Oxford: Oxford University Press.

Padden, Carol. 1980. The Deaf Community and the Culture of Deaf People. In Baker and Battison eds., *Sign Language and the Deaf Community: Essays in Honor of William C. Stokoe.* Silver Spring, MD: National Association of the Deaf.

_____ and Tom Humphries. 1988. *Deaf In America: Voices From A Culture.* Cambridge: Harvard.

_____ and Harry Markowicz. 1976. Cultural Conflicts Between Hearing and Deaf Communities. In F. B. and A. B. Crammatte, eds. *Proceedings of the VII World Congress of the World Federation of the Deaf.* Washington, D.C.: National Association of the Deaf.

Peet, H. 1859. Words Not 'Representatives' of Signs, but of Ideas. *American Annals of the Deaf* 11:1-8.

Propp, Vladimir. 1968. *Morphology of the Folktale.* Austin: University of Texas Press.

Radcliff-Brown, A. R. 1940. On Joking Relationships. *Africa* 13:195-210.

Rainer, J., K. Altschuler and F. Kallman, eds. 1963. *Family and Mental Health Problems in a Deaf Population.* New York: Department of Genetics, New York State Psychiatric Institute, Columbia University.

Rodda, Michael. 1982. An Analysis of the Myth that Mainstreaming and Integration are Synonymous. In Boros and Stuckless, eds. *Social Change and Deaf People, Working Papers No. 6, Conference: Sociology of Deafness,* Washington, D.C.: Gallaudet College.

Rose, Peter. 1968. *The Subject is Race.* New York: Oxford University Press.

_____. 1981. *They and We.* 4th Edition, New York: Random House.

Royce, Anya Peterson. 1982. *Ethnic Identity: Strategies of Diversity.* Bloomington: Indiana University Press.

Rutherford, Susan D. 1988. The Culture of American Deaf People. *Sign Language Studies,* 59: 129-147.

_____.1982. Slurred Name Signs. Unpublished manuscript.

_____.and Sheila Jacobs, eds. 1986. *The C.O.D.A. Experience.* Proceedings of the First National CODA Conference for Hearing Children of Deaf Adults. Santa Barbara: C.O.D.A. Organization.

Sagarin, Edward. 1971. From the Ethnic Minorities to the Other Minorities. In Edward Sagarin, ed. *The Other Minorities.* Waltham, MA: Ginn & Co. 1-20.

San Francisco Public Library, Susan D. Rutherford Project Producer. 1984. *American Culture: The Deaf Perspective Video Series.* "Deaf Folklore," "Deaf Heritage," Deaf Literature," and "Minorities in the Deaf Community." 3/4" & 1/2" VHS, 30 min. each.

Schein, Jerome D. 1968. *The Deaf Community.* Washington, D.C.: Gallaudet College Press.

_____ and Marcus Delk. 1974. *The Deaf Population in the United States.* Silver Spring, MD: National Association of the Deaf.

Schermerhorn, Richard. 1970. *Comparative Ethnic Relations.* New York: Random House.

Schlesinger, Hilde. 1972. Meaning and Enjoyment: Language Acquisition in Deaf Children. In T. J. O'Rourke, ed. *Psycholinguistics and Total Communication: The State of the Art.* Washington, D. C.: American Annals of the Deaf: 92-102.

_____ and Katheryn Meadow. 1972. *Sound and Sign: Childhood Deafness and Mental Health.* Berkeley: University of California Press.

Schwartzman, Helen B. 1978. *Transformations: The Anthropology of Children's Play.* New York: Plenum Press.

Scofield, Sandra J. 1978. The Language Delayed Child in the

Mainstream Primary Classroom. *Language Arts*. 55 6:719-725.

Siegel, J. 1969. The Enlightenment and the Evolution of a Language of Signs in France and England. *Journal of the History of Ideas*. 30:96-115.

Spicer, Edward H. 1971. Persistent Cultural Systems: A Comparative Study of Identity Systems That Can Adapt to Constrasting Environments. *Science* 174, 4011:795-800.

Stephenson, Richard M. 1951. Conflict and Control, Functions of Humor. *American Journal of Sociology*. 56:560-574.

Stokoe, William. 1960. *Sign Language Structure: An Outline of the Visual Communication System of the American Deaf*. Buffalo: University of Buffalo, Occasional Paper 8.

_____. 1970. Sign Language Diglossia. *Studies in Linguistics* 21:27-41.

_____, ed. 1980. *Sign and Culture: A Reader for Students of ASL*. Silver Spring, MD: Linstok Press.

_____. , H. Bernard and Carol Padden. 1976. An Elite Group In Deaf Society. *Sign Language Studies* 12:189-210.

_____, Dorothy Casterline and Carl Cronenberg. 1965. *A Dictionary of American Sign Language*. Washington, D.C.: Gallaudet Press.

Smith, Cheri, Ella Mae Lentz and Ken Mikos. 1988. *Signing Naturally Teacher's Curriculum Guide* and *Student Videotext & Workbook*. San Diego: Dawn Sign Press.

Supalla, Sam. 1992. *The Book of Name Signs: Naming in American Sign Language*. San Diego: Dawn Sign Press.

Sutton-Smith, Brian. 1972. *The Folkgames of Children*. Austin: University of Texas Press.

Tedlock, Dennis. 1971. On the Translation of Style in Oral Narrative. *Journal of American Folklore* 84:114-33.

Toelken, Barre. 1979. *The Dynamics of Folklore*. Boston: Houghton Mifflin.

Trybus, Raymond. 1980. Sign Language, Power and Mental Health. In Baker and Battison, eds. *Sign Language and the Deaf Community*. Silver Spring, MD: National Association of the Deaf, 201-220.

Turner, Victor. 1974. Liminal to Liminoid, in Play, Flow and Ritual. *Rice University Studies* 60:53-92.

Vernon, McCay and Bernard Makowsky. 1968. Deafness and Minority Group Dynamics. *The Deaf American* 21:3-6.

Winefield, Richard. 1987. *Never The Twain Shall Meet: Bell, Gallaudet, and The Communications Debate*. Washington: Gallaudet University Press.

Winick, Charles. 1976. The Social Contexts of Humor. In Laughing Matter? A Symposium of Studies on Humor as Communication. *Journal of Communication* 26:124-128.

Wolfenstein, Martha. 1954. *Children's Humor*. Glencoe: Free Press. Repr. Bloomington: Indiana University Press, 1978.

Woodward, James. 1973a. Some Observations on Sociolinguistic Variation and American Sign Language. *Kansas Journal of Sociology* 9:191-199.

_____. 1973b. Some Characteristics of Pidgin Sign English. *Sign Language Studies* 3:39-46.

_____. 1973c. Implicational Lects on the Deaf Diglossic Continnum. Ph.D. dissertation, Georgetown University.

_____. 1973d. Interrule Implication on American Sign Language. *Sign Language Studies* 3:47-56.

_____. 1979. *Signs of Sexual Behavior*. Silver Spring, MD: T. J. Publishing.

_____. 1982. *How You Gonna Get to Heaven if You Can't Talk With Jesus: The Educational Establishment vs. The Deaf Community*. Silver Spring, MD: T. J. Publishers.

_____ and Carol Erting. 1975. Synchronic Variation and Historical Change in American Sign Language. *Language Sciences* 37:9-12.

_____ and Harry Markowicz. 1980. Some Handy New Ideas on Pidgins and Creoles: Pidgin Sign Languages. In William Stokoe, ed. *Sign and Culture*. Silver Spring, MD: Linstok Press.

DATE DUE

4/21/04	ILL 4209350		
NOV 22 04			
3·22·13	100603604		

WITHDRAWN FROM
BLUEGRASS COMMUNITY
& TECHNICAL COLLEGE

Printed in USA

HIGHSMITH #45230